DATE			

Could It Be
Autism?

Could It Be
Autism?

A Parent's Guide to the
First Signs and Next Steps

Nancy D. Wiseman,
Founder and President, First Signs, Inc.
with *Kim Painter Koffsky*

A Lark Production
Broadway Books
New York

BROADWAY

Broadway Books titles may be purchased for business or promotional use or for special sales. For information, please write to: Special Markets Department, Random House, Inc., 1745 Broadway, New York, NY 10019.

PRINTED IN THE UNITED STATES OF AMERICA

BROADWAY BOOKS and its logo, a letter B bisected on the diagonal, are trademarks of Random House, Inc.

Visit our website at www.broadwaybooks.com

First edition published 2006

Book design by Michael Collica

Library of Congress Cataloging-in-Publication Data
    Wiseman, Nancy D.
        Could it be autism? : a parent's guide to the first signs and next steps / Nancy D. Wiseman.—1st ed.
            p.   cm.
        Includes index.
        1. Autism. I. Title.

    RC553.A88W57 2006
    616.85'882—dc22   2005050756

ISBN 0-7679-1972-6

10   9   8   7   6   5   4   3   2   1

For Sarah, my eternal source of love and inspiration. Together we can overcome any obstacle. And for all the professionals who see the hope in our children and bring us closer to the dreams we once thought would be forgotten. In memory of Dr. Robert H. Wharton, our beloved developmental pediatrician, who had the courage and conviction to fight for his patients and their families.

Foreword

Only thirty years ago, the diagnosis of autism was based on such obvious signs as a complete lack of eye contact, rocking back and forth, and hand-flapping in children five years and older. Few of us were comfortable making the diagnosis before this age because early signs were not yet specifically categorized, nor was the value of early intervention established. In recent years, as our understanding of child development has increased, we've focused on more subtle differences earlier in life, particularly in communication and social-emotional development.

While our knowledge of child development is constantly increasing, financial pressure from insurers to see more patients in less time has prevented systematic and more sophisticated screening. *Less than half* of pediatricians provide any form of developmental screening, and only half of those use a structured screening tool. The role of parents as good observers of child development and behavior and as advocates for their children remains essential. If parents have information they are more likely to be effective partners with pediatricians and others in identifying children with social-emotional problems, as well as more likely to contribute to the child's treatment. Knowledge of child development should go beyond an early identification of problems to include an understanding and appreciation of the individuality of each child and the entire family and other caregivers.

The message "wait and see" is understandably a battle cry to parents whose children seem to have problems. The social-emotional growth of children can branch off in many directions—to diagnoses such as developmental delay, autism, or Asperger syndrome—or simply to a child with a certain temperament. My own daughter in the first six months of life was a very "good" baby; she hardly ever cried. But on the flip side, we had to stand on our heads to get a little bit of a smile, and she never laughed. Her low intensity of response and slow-to-warm-up style were a real concern to us, and we discussed whether she possibly could have autism. Her development proceeded normally, but she was a shy child until late in high school. Children who have temperaments like my daughter's may comprise 5 to 10 percent of all children. For them, that "wait and see" attitude is appropriate—given a lot of professional support in the meantime. However, wait and see without any support is never appropriate. Whether a child will ultimately have a developmental problem, or is just slow to warm up, parents and other caregivers need information. Intervention starts with parental concern and concrete advice on how to promote a child's development. If the child has a developmental problem, parents need very specific strategies that go beyond the "good enough" parenting that is effective for most children.

Early on, even a sophisticated evaluation may not identify what will become more obvious six months or a year later. Sometimes parents can be reassured because their expectations for development are inappropriate. On the other hand, it is incumbent on the physician to refer a child to someone with greater knowledge and skills for further evaluation. During the time until the diagnosis is made, parents benefit from strategies to promote their child's development. Many strategies are intuitive, and frequently parents don't give themselves enough credit for being able to read their child's signals and keep them engaged in communication or other activities. All parents, however, can use more information so they can contribute not only to the early and timely identification of a problem, but also to intervention and ongoing education for pediatricians.

Physicians have legitimate concerns about categorizing or diagnosing children with a disability because of the potentially self-fulfilling nature of labels. A diagnosis can significantly affect what happens to a child. Sometimes it opens doors to services and experiences that a child needs to reach her developmental potential. Failure to get a timely diagnosis and intervention can impair a child's ability to reach his or her potential. The question of whether to diagnose or not remains a strong concern of parents and professionals alike, even though everyone wants what's best for the child. Education and information for professionals and parents are crucial in order to counteract the possible stigma attached to certain diagnoses.

This book is a wonderful first step in providing just the kind of thoughtful, accessible, expert information anyone concerned about a child needs. My hope is that the book will fuel a revolution that will help parents, physicians, and other professionals share the knowledge necessary to understand how best to help all children grow to their full potential.

Barry S. Zuckerman, M.D.

This book is the result of my personal journey with my daughter, Sarah. Without her, this book and First Signs would not exist. I wish to thank Sarah for sharing her love, her mommy's time, and her story so openly—and for showing me that just about anything is possible. I wish to thank my mom and stepdad, Beverly and Peter Eagleson, for always being there for us throughout this journey, no matter how bumpy it gets. My heartfelt thanks to my mom for pushing me to get Sarah's diagnosis and for her contribution to this book.

My deepest gratitude and admiration to Sarah's invaluable team of doctors, therapists, and educators, who helped us get where we are today and who I trust will help us get where we need to go tomorrow: Brenda Braunmiller and our team at Pentucket Early Intervention; Dr. Karen Levine and our team at Building Blocks; Beth Doerr; Tara Savoie and our team at OTA Wakefield; our teams at the NorthShore Education Consortium and Pentucket Regional School District; Wendy Osgood, Dr. Ann Densmore, Dr. Lars Lundgren, Dr. Timothy Buie, Kelly Dorfman, Dr. Raphael Castro, Dr. Ira Glovinsky, Dr. Margaret Bauman, Dr. Janet Wozniak, Dr. Kenneth Bock and his staff at the Rhinebeck Health Center; and Dr. Stanley Greenspan.

My sincere gratitude to my clinical advisory board for their ongoing support and invaluable contribution to this book and to the First Signs organization: Dr. Margaret Bauman, Dr. Geraldine

Dawson, Kelly Dorfman, Dr. Frances Glascoe, Dr. Stanley Greenspan, Dr. Harold Ireton, Dr. Rebecca Landa, Dr. Catherine Lord, Dr. Barry Prizant, Dr. Ricki Robinson, Dr. Amy Wetherby, Dr. Serena Wieder, and Dr. Barry Zuckerman.

To the many organizations and individuals that have funded First Signs over the years, thank you for your generous support and contributions. Thank you, Laura Straus, for allowing First Signs to use your beautiful black-and-white photographs of children. And to past and present board members of First Signs, Inc., thank you for your generous contribution of your time and effort: Ilene Beal, Andrée Cordella, Elaine Gabovitch, Dr. Karen Levine, and Dr. Robert W. Wharton (now deceased).

Many other professionals and parents contributed to the development of this book. A special thanks to all those individuals who provided stories, quotes, tips, advice, and suggestions (a few parent names have been changed to protect their children). Their insight and wisdom have been invaluable. These individuals include: Kathie and Carl Tomczuk, Ron and Sharon Oberleitner, Penny Kelly, Beth and Frank Scott, Kathy Bauer, Becky Wilson, Susan Sutherland, Ellen and Gary Weitzen, Brenda Eaton, Gail Tino, Peter Bell, Julia O'Connor, Rhonda Twitty, Karin Cather, Fred Wayne, Beth Corcoran, Mary Barbera, Joy Johnson, Ann Guay, Debra Egan, Ida Palmieri, Arlene Cohen, Danielle Draut, Raina Rosenblum, Katherine Flaschen, Jean Rossettie, Wendy Osgood, Samahria Lyte Kaufman, Don Meyer, Dr. Anne Holmes, Dr. Karen Levine, Dr. Ira Glovinsky, Dr. Janet Wozniak, Dr. Kenneth Bock, and Dr. Robert Naseef.

I am especially grateful to Lisa DiMona of Lark Productions for finding me, convincing me to write this book, and for keeping me going with her great sense of humor and easygoing style; to Trish Medved of Broadway Books for believing in me and for being such a wonderful editor; and to Kim Painter Koffsky for her amazing contribution, dedication, and endless hours (and to her family— Dan, Ethan, and Sam Koffsky—for letting me borrow so much of Kim's time). This book was, in every sense, true teamwork and a labor of love.

Contents

At first, I didn't notice the signs. Only later, when I looked back at videotapes of my daughter, could I see it. Sarah was happy and engaged, sometimes. She smiled and laughed with us; she responded to our voices and faces. But at other times, I saw a faraway look. I saw myself and my husband working very hard—too hard, I realize now—to get another smile, another glance from our sweet, quiet baby.

Gradually, as the signs became more obvious, as the moments of connection dwindled, I began to worry about Sarah. She had stopped babbling and started to refuse my hugs and avoid my gaze. She used her few words like obsessive mantras—chanting "Shoes, shoes, shoes" as she stared into her daddy's open closet and saying "Cheese" and "Cough" over and over, for no apparent reason at all. But it wasn't until Sarah was twenty-three months old, after months of "Wait and see" from our pediatrician, that I learned my daughter had serious developmental delays. Several months after that, the news got worse: Sarah had a form of autism.

In spite of the needless wait we experienced, Sarah was diagnosed quite early and treated effectively. Today, she is nine years old and, though she still faces challenges, she has made remarkable progress. She is one of the lucky ones.

I wrote this book because I want you and your children to be just as lucky.

I want to share with you what scientists now know about the earliest signs of autism and other disorders that could affect your child's ability to communicate and connect. If you are already concerned about your child's development, I want to teach you how to translate your concerns into action—action that will get your child the best, fastest help possible. Finally, I want to offer hope: every parent worried about autism and other developmental disorders needs to know that children who get early, intense, individualized treatment can make great progress.

Sadly, a growing number of parents need this advice. Two decades ago, autism—a disorder that affects a child's ability to communicate, relate, play, imagine, and learn—was thought to affect one in 5,000 children. Today, the federal Centers for Disease Control and Prevention (CDC) estimates that one in every 166 children has a form of autism. And autism isn't the only worry. Studies at the CDC suggest one child in six today will be diagnosed with some developmental or behavioral disability. This rather stunning apparent increase in children in developmental peril is unexplained. It is frightening.

I hear the fear every day, in the phone calls and e-mails I get from parents who have learned about First Signs, Inc., the national nonprofit organization I started to ensure that more children are effectively screened, evaluated, and treated for autism and other developmental disorders. These parents are worried about their children, but don't know whether their worries are justified. Many, having read and heard so much about autism in recent years, specifically want to know whether their child might have autism—and, if not, what else might be wrong.

So, if you are a parent concerned about a child—especially a baby, toddler, or preschooler—this book is for you. And I hope you will share this information with other parents and with pediatricians, preschool teachers, child care workers, grandparents, and others who work with young children. In doing so, you will help me to expand the work of First Signs.

The First Signs Story

This is an endeavor that started in my head several years ago as I commuted three hours each day, to and from my job running a communications department for a major corporation near Boston. I was forty-one years old, married, and had a two-year-old daughter who was diagnosed with pervasive developmental disorder–not otherwise specified (PDD-NOS), a form of autism. I realized the last thing I wanted to do was to spend three hours each day in a car. I wanted to be with my daughter. And I wanted to do work that mattered. My successful career had come complete with a six-figure salary, a nanny, and an impressive house overlooking the Merrimack River. But I did not have what I wanted most—the time and freedom to do everything in my power to help Sarah and other children in developmental trouble.

I knew other families needed help because, in the course of having Sarah diagnosed and started with treatment, I had learned some alarming facts. First, I learned that most pediatricians and other doctors know shockingly little about social and emotional development. And I learned that, despite the urging of professional groups and scientists, most do not formally and routinely screen children for signs of developmental delay. Instead, many rely on casual observation and hunches. Others do some screening, but use ineffective methods. As a result, they initially miss the vast majority of children with delays and disorders. When pediatricians do see and acknowledge developmental delays in young children, they often tell parents, "Wait and see"—advice that runs counter to everything we know about the value of early intervention. They also commonly pass on myths: boys develop much later than girls, they say; silence or odd play habits may be signs of genius ("Einstein was a late talker, you know"). Rarely are children in trouble quickly referred for expert evaluation and treatment. The result: despite the fact that 17 percent of children will eventually be diagnosed with some behavioral or developmental disability, a mere 2 percent of children under age three are enrolled in state-funded Early Intervention programs.* Up to 80 percent of children with disabilities get no help before kindergarten. When the problem is autism, diagnosis typically occurs between ages three and six, even though unmistakable signs are usually present in the first eighteen months. Experts say almost any child with an autism-related disorder can be diagnosed by age two, which is early enough for effective therapy to change the course of many children's lives.

And so, I quit my corporate job and set out to do a more important one.

After officially founding First Signs in 2000, I learned even more. For starters, I learned that there are many wonderful pediatricians, family physicians, and nurse practitioners out there. A few already do a great job of screening children for developmental delays. Others are eager to learn how. They've told me about the obstacles they face—including ridiculously short appointment times, a lack of insurance reimbursement, and a lack of training in developmental screening. I knew I couldn't have an immediate impact on the time and insurance problems, which are part of our country's broader health care crisis, but with my marketing background, I could do something about the training of physicians and other health care workers. I could also help to educate the wider public—including parents, educators, and child care workers—about the urgent need for earlier recognition of children with developmental disorders.

And so, I've been busy. Backed by a team of expert advisers, First Signs has launched programs to educate parents and professionals in several states. We've received requests to start similar programs

*Part C of Individuals with Disabilities Education Improvement Act of 2004 (IDEA) provides states with funds to assist in maintaining and implementing "a statewide, comprehensive, coordinated, multidisciplinary, interagency system to provide early intervention services for infants and toddlers with disabilities and their families."

in most other states and in five countries. I have personally spoken before more than 15,000 medical professionals, clinicians, educators, parents, and government officials, at more than fifty conferences, training seminars, and other events. And research shows First Signs has had an impact. Data collected after the first phase of our Minnesota program showed that between 2002 and 2003, autism spectrum diagnoses rose 23 percent among children under age twenty-one—and an astonishing 75 percent among children aged two and under.

Even as First Signs has grown in scope and reach, I've continued to see it as a personal mission. On many late nights, I am still at my computer, exchanging e-mails with parents who are worried about their children. Again and again I hear from mothers and fathers who just know something is wrong, but who can't get the help they need from their doctors, their communities, or even their families. These parents want to do the right thing. But they don't know what it is.

About This Book

This book will tell you what to do if you are concerned about your child's development and then what to do if your concerns turn out to be justified. You will learn how to get a diagnosis, if one is warranted, and how to design and launch the best intervention plan—a plan that is based on your child's "unique developmental profile," a concept developed by Stanley I. Greenspan. Dr. Greenspan, who is an adviser to First Signs, practices psychiatry in Bethesda, Maryland; he treats children with developmental delays and has written many books on early child development.

- In Part I, you'll learn how to become an effective advocate for your child and why it's so important to diagnose and treat developmental problems as early as possible. You'll have an opportunity to assess your child's social, emotional, and communication development with the First

Signs Developmental Milestone Checklist. You'll also learn about Red Flags—signs that mean a child needs immediate evaluation.

- In Part II, you'll learn the specific steps you must take to confirm or rule out a developmental delay or disorder. You'll learn to how to get a diagnosis and, even more important, a detailed developmental profile of your child. You'll also learn how to connect with the professionals who can help you and your child through this process.
- In Part III, you'll learn how to get the further information and support you need and the individualized treatment your child needs after a diagnosis. This section includes a detailed list of available treatments.
- In Part IV, you'll learn what to expect as your child grows and how families cope and continue to advocate for their children, and often for others, in the months and years after a diagnosis.

Some parents will read the first several chapters of this book with a growing sense of relief, concluding that their children probably do not have autism or any other developmental disorder. If that happens to you, I hope you'll have new confidence in your ability to recognize and act on signs of trouble should they arise in the future. Other parents will read with a growing sense of alarm, as they realize that their children are missing important developmental milestones or exhibiting Red Flags for developmental delay (detailed in Chapter 3). In either case, I urge you to share what you learn with your child's doctor. If your child appears to be on a healthy developmental track, you can safeguard that healthy development by demanding that, from now on, your child be routinely, thoroughly screened by a health care professional. If you conclude that your child may be in developmental trouble, time is of the essence: please follow the guidelines in this book and get professional help right away.

This book will be of greatest interest to parents who are concerned about a very young child who does not seem to be communicating or connecting with the world around her. These are the core signs of autism and related disorders. If you are troubled because your baby doesn't babble or look at faces, your toddler doesn't speak or gesture, or your preschooler doesn't know how to play or hold a conversation, this book provides vital guidance. If your child is meeting a lot of milestones, but still seems socially and emotionally out of sync with his peers, this book will give you the detailed information you need to either put your fears to rest or pursue your concerns. Those parents who already are worried about a specific disorder, especially autism, will find out exactly how to confirm or rule out that diagnosis.

Keep in mind that some children who show early but mild signs of developmental delay never get a specific diagnosis, though they certainly may benefit from early intervention. Also keep in mind that a child can end up with more than one diagnosis—or a completely different diagnosis than parents or professionals first suspect. So this book isn't just about autism. When a very young child has trouble communicating and connecting, there are many possible diagnoses, among them:

- autism spectrum disorders (including Asperger syndrome and PDD-NOS)
- speech and language disorders
- attention deficit hyperactivity disorder (ADHD)
- sensory integration dysfunction
- mental health disorders (including anxiety and mood disorders)
- certain genetic syndromes
- mental retardation
- learning disabilities

A more complete, detailed list of possible diagnoses is provided in Chapter 6. Although this book is not specifically targeted to families whose children are born with clear developmental challenges (such as those with Down syndrome or other quickly apparent disabilities), it also can be of use to them. The information on how to get the most out of Early Intervention programs, school systems, therapy, and other kinds of support should be relevant to any parent of an infant, toddler, or preschooler with a developmental delay or disorder. What if you are worried about a somewhat older child? There's information here for you, too. Children don't stop developing at age three—and interventions don't stop working then, either. No matter how old your child is, he deserves the best care possible.

I want to briefly mention three things you won't find in this book:

- An opinion about the likely cause of the recent apparent increase in autism and other developmental disorders. That burning topic is well covered in many other places.
- An endorsement of any particular therapy. I'll tell you what worked for Sarah and give some special attention to Floortime, a therapy that was the center of her treatment. But I'll also feature the stories of other families who used different methods, with apparently great results.
- A claim that, with the right therapies, you can "cure" any child of autism or related disorders. As you'll read, some children, like Sarah, do remarkably well and, at some point, no longer qualify for their original diagnoses. Most others make significant progress, but continue to need varying amounts of help and support. A few, for reasons that are poorly understood, make little or no progress, despite intensive therapy.

What lies in your own child's future? No parent knows that. The best that you can do is to care for your child and give him what he needs to reach his full potential. The catch, of course, is that different children need different things. So look to your child. Find out what he needs. That's what this book is all about.

Part One
Early Signs

Is your child on a healthy developmental path? Or is she headed for trouble? If you are holding your baby in your arms right now or watching your toddler play, the answers could be right before your eyes. The earliest signs that a child is withdrawing from the social world, struggling with emotional regulation, or failing to learn basic communication skills can be easy to recognize once you know what they are. In fact, researchers know that many of the danger signs are the very ones that often trouble parents months or years before a child is formally diagnosed with a developmental delay or disorder. They are the very things a parent worries about when a baby seems distant or unresponsive, an eighteen-month-old is not talking, or a three-year-old is not playing with other children. The first challenge is to close that gap: to harness the observational power of parents and the knowledge of scientists to get children the earliest help possible. Over the next few chapters, you'll learn how to do your part as a parent to make sure your child's development gets the attention it deserves.

Chapter One

You Make a Difference

Y ou are a parent, not a doctor or a scientist.

But, when it comes to your child, you are an expert. You know that little face and whether it lights up when you walk into a room. You know your baby's babbling, burbling voice and would be the first to notice if it suddenly fell silent. You know how your toddler behaves when he sees a new toy, meets a new child, goes to a birthday party, or visits a shopping mall. You know what makes her cry and what makes her laugh. And, while your pediatrician has seen hundreds of sore throats and infected ears, you've seen a few things, too. You've seen children playing in parks and squabbling at family dinners. You've seen babies playing peek-a-boo and preschoolers playing house. And you wouldn't be a parent if you had not compared your child to those children—if you had not noticed how your child resembles them and differs from them.

Of course, not every difference is a disorder. Far from it. But if your instincts are telling you something is wrong—that something about your child is quite different from other children or that something essential about your child has changed or become increasingly troubling, your instincts are probably right.

You Know When Something Is Wrong

As part of my work with First Signs, I've spent a lot of time talking with doctors and researchers about the differences between young children with developmental delays and those without them. Time and time again they tell me about one crucial difference. Children with developmental delays have parents who are persistently worried about them. So, if you are worried about how your child is developing, how he or she is learning and behaving, you should take your worry seriously. It could be a warning sign.

> Parents have been diagnosing their children from early on. They know it, they feel it. They say to me all the time, "I just know something's just not right . . . the way he does this or the way he does that . . ." And they're right, usually.
>
> Anne Holmes, director of outreach services at Eden
> Family of Services, Princeton, N J.

All parents worry about their children sometimes. All occasionally need some reassurance that the quirks they see are just that. One survey found that 70 percent of parents in pediatric waiting rooms had questions about their children's development or behavior. When something really is wrong, though, the worry does not go away. The child's differences don't go away, either. Usually they just become more apparent, more troubling.

Some parents whose children are eventually diagnosed with autism or other developmental disorders realize that their children are different as babies. A few notice specific, clear-cut problems; many others have nagging, vague concerns that are harder to express.

> From the day I brought him home from the hospital, I knew there was something going on. He couldn't feed, he couldn't suck a bottle. And, as a toddler, he couldn't give

kisses. He would go to kiss me and would just bang his face into my mouth.

Kathy Bauer of Pennsylvania, mother of Andy,
diagnosed with speech apraxia at age three

She was five or six months old when I first started feeling something wasn't right. But I couldn't put my finger on it. I felt like I was bonding to her, but she wasn't bonding to me.

Becky Wilson of Oregon, mother of Zoë, diagnosed
at age four with developmental language disorder
and "regulatory disorder with autistic behaviors"

Other parents see signs accumulate over time or appear suddenly, often between the first and second year of a child's life.

When Evan was fifteen months old I noticed he wasn't behaving like other children of his age. . . . He wasn't interacting with the world like other kids.

Susan Sutherland of Massachusetts, mother of Evan,
diagnosed with PDD-NOS just before age three

When doctors ask the right questions, worried parents almost always speak up. And, once their child is diagnosed with a problem, even those parents who do not express their worries at first usually say that they knew "something was wrong." Often they "just burst into tears" when their fears are confirmed, one researcher says. "They will say, 'I was worried about my child, but I thought I was just being an anxious parent.'"

Studies show that parents of all educational, cultural, and economic backgrounds are able to recognize developmental warning signs. Where do parents get this amazing power of prediction? From observing their child and the children around them.

Pediatricians see a child for about fifteen minutes during a "well" visit. Parents see their children every day, all day, in all sorts of settings. They also see other children, alone and in groups, in the grocery store, at church, even in the pediatric waiting room. They see siblings, cousins, playmates, and neighbors. Everywhere they go, they compare and notice how their child is like other children and how he or she is different.

> I remember when my daughter was eighteen months old, you'd say, "Go close the door," and she'd go close the door. My son had no receptive language. If you said, "Go close the door," he'd just stand there.
>
> *Brenda Eaton of Pennsylvania, mother of Brendan,*
> *diagnosed with autism at age three*

> If you're around children all the time, you realize the way they can communicate without even saying a word. He didn't have that at a year or eighteen months.
>
> *Ellen Weitzen of New Jersey, mother of Chris,*
> *diagnosed with autism at age three*

One clinical professor I know used to train young pediatricians to recognize developmental disorders. Sometimes she would send her trainees to day care centers and schools so that they could see what parents see all the time—children playing, talking, and learning together. She told me about one trainee who was not convinced that a five-year-old with a technically normal but lower than average IQ needed special help. The young doctor was sent to a day care center, where he observed typical four- and five-year-olds at play. That did the trick. He quickly saw that the child with the apparently okay test scores was lagging far behind in speech. The child was not okay at all.

Finding a Professional Partner

Still, you may believe that what you know about your child pales in comparison to what seasoned pediatricians, family physicians, and nurse practitioners know about the science of development. If you've taken your child to every routine checkup and gotten a clean bill of health, you may feel that's reassurance enough. Unfortunately, that's not the case. While most health professionals do a good job of assessing physical development and try to measure cognitive growth, far too few know how to assess social and emotional development or how to interpret the early behavioral signs of disorders like autism. Some well-meaning doctors ask about these topics, but use the wrong questions. Others rely on their own, too-brief observations. And, unfortunately, far too few children with developmental delays and disorders get the early, intensive help that could put them on a healthier path.

The good news is that you can do something about this. You already know a lot about your child. You are about to learn a lot more about how to assess your child's social and emotional development and how to get prompt help if it's needed. To take full advantage of the advice in this book, though, you also need at least one professional partner. For most parents, that partner will initially be a pediatrician or family physician.

> Parents might know something is wrong, but we don't know what, and it's really up to the pediatrician to help us.
> *Gary Weitzen of New Jersey, father of Chris,*
> *diagnosed with autism at age three*

In an ideal world, you'd already have a virtual T. Berry Brazelton on your personal team. Like the legendary child care guru, your child's pediatrician would be someone who believes in taking care of whole children and whole families, not just broken legs and sore throats. That doctor also would be well trained in child development and thoroughly up-to-date on the latest research in developmental disorders and how to detect them. She would find a way to fit routine developmental screening into her practice. And she would refer every child with developmental delays to other appropriate professionals for immediate evaluation and help. When parents had trouble getting past long waiting lists or finding the right specialist, she would do all she could to help cut through the red tape.

There are some doctors like that. In fact, the best pediatricians I know say that being an advocate for parents and children is an essential part of their jobs. They expect to spend part of their workday helping families connect with other professionals and other services. They make it their business to know what assistance is available in their communities.

These same pediatricians take seriously their responsibility to follow a child's development. They are not annoyed or put on the defensive when parents, often armed with questions gleaned from a stack of books, want to talk about their children's social and emotional development.

If your child's current doctor lacks these qualities, you are at a great disadvantage. You will find it much harder to sort out your worries about your child and, if needed, get expert, timely help. So, before you go much further, it may be time to shop for a new pediatrician or family physician.

Maybe, like me, you carefully picked your child's current doctor even before your baby was born. I remember visiting four pediatricians during the final weeks of my pregnancy and feeling that I'd been very thorough in my search. I asked about things like office hours and support for breastfeeding and picked a doctor I felt I could call in the middle of a three A.M. crisis. But I found out that my carefully chosen, highly recommended pediatrician was not too pleased with my three A.M. phone calls. My second pediatrician was great about middle-of-the-night phone calls, but did not recognize that my daughter was in developmental trouble.

I eventually found a more knowledgeable pediatrician. And so can you. Ask other parents for recommendations. When you hear of a good prospect, schedule a time to go in and talk with him or her, preferably without your child along. If you choose a practice and later become dissatisfied, try again. This process can be time-consuming, but will be well worthwhile, especially if your child has a developmental delay. Ideally, you will find a pediatric practice where:

- developmental screening and observation are a routine part of every well-child visit.
- doctors are well informed and eager to discuss development. When you go for that consultation, ask questions like "What do you look for at each stage of development?"; "During a typical visit, when and how do you check development?"; and "Where do you refer children with developmental difficulties?"
- doctors get to know the children under their care. That means that your child usually sees the same physician or nurse practitioner, whether for sick or well visits. If it's a large practice, be sure to ask whether you can pick a particular doctor and stick with her.
- doctors are accessible, and not only in emergencies. They take phone calls every day or answer e-mails from patients.
- other staff members are accessible and helpful. Believe me, one helpful receptionist or nurse can make a huge difference should your child need complicated care.

One caveat: while it would be great if all of us had many pediatricians to choose from, your insurance policy may limit your choices and so may geography. Some parents are lucky enough to live in big metropolitan areas with many competing doctors, but others live in rural communities where just one or two doctors serve families for many miles around. If that's your situation, you may have to work especially hard to get what your child needs.

It Comes Down to You

The truth remains that no matter how good your pediatrician is, you are your child's best observer and greatest champion. You are the gatekeeper, the person who stands between your child and the rest of the world, deciding which experiences and people to invite in and which to try to keep out. For parents of typically developing children, being a gatekeeper means choosing the best preschool or the most nurturing nanny. It might mean banning certain TV shows or toys.

Parents' Rights

First Signs believes that if you are a parent concerned about your child's development, you have a right to

- share concerns with health care providers and educators
- be listened to and taken seriously
- get developmental screening for your child at every well visit
- have time to ask questions and express concerns, even if that means scheduling extra meetings or appointments
- get quick follow-up appointments
- see a specialist for a full evaluation
- seek a second opinion
- get answers to all of your questions about development and about your child
- participate in major decisions about your child's care and education
- know all the treatment and educational options available when a problem is found
- change doctors when you are dissatisfied and get complete records transferred to new doctors
- get copies of any of your child's medical records
- request an interpreter if any provider does not speak your language
- protect your family's privacy

For parents whose children turn out to have developmental challenges, being a gatekeeper means all that and much more. It means choosing the people who can best help you and your child to navigate an often uncertain path toward the best possible outcome. It means working with those people to decide what is best for your child, but often making the final decisions yourself. It means becoming a true advocate.

If you have picked up this book, you are already thinking about how to be a better advocate for your child. Even if your child turns out to have no developmental problems, you will find yourself advocating for many years to come—working with doctors, teachers, coaches, and others to get what's best for your son or daughter. If your child does have a delay or disorder, your duties will be even more demanding. You may find yourself negotiating with developmental psychologists, pediatric neurologists, school administrators, and veritable armies of therapists. And you may be overwhelmed at times with all the treatment options and conflicting opinions about what is right for your child. You may feel you've been assigned a job for which you are ill qualified.

Never forget, you are uniquely qualified. You know more, and care more, about your child than anyone else. You are the only one who can make sure he gets what he needs from the larger world. All you require is a little more information and a few more skills. So, learn more about why it's so important to act on your concerns—and then take action. Your child is depending on you.

To Do Now

If you are concerned about a child, get out a piece of paper, right now. Write down your exact concerns. If you've noticed your child isn't smiling, make a note of whether she smiled in the past and when. If you think she's stopped babbling, write down the sounds she used to make—"Da-da?" "Ba-ba?"—and when you think she stopped. If you can think of a particular incident that troubled you—the day she wandered away from you at the grocery store, the time she had a tantrum over taking a different path back from the park—describe it in detail.

If your concerns are vague, write down the best description you can muster. What is it about your child that seems different or troubling?

You are taking the first step toward compiling your child's developmental history—a history that, in the days ahead, will help find the best help for you and your child.

Chapter Two

Why Early Detection Matters

By now, you've heard it: the first three years of a child's life are critical. Newborn brains may come fully stocked with neurons, but it is early experience that really puts those brain cells to work, making connections that last a lifetime.

A baby starts life with about 100 billion brain cells. Between birth and age three, those cells connect with one another at a furious rate. Each time a child hears a loud voice, feels a soft blanket, sees a bold pattern, or tastes a sweet food, a connection is made or reinforced. The connections used most often become permanent; those rarely or never used are lost.

In the crudest terms, babies and toddlers must use it or lose it. While the truth is a little more complicated, for a child's developing brain, the importance of the first three years is real. During this brief period, the brain is developing its capacity for everything from vision to speech to muscle control. And, just as important, it is developing the ability to think and feel deeply.

What happens is amazing. Your baby is born and, very quickly, learns the sound of your voice. She learns to recognize your face, and soon is sharing long, adoring looks with you. A dance of learning and love has begun. And the baby who is engaged with the people around her learns so much: she learns that faces can tell a thousand tales and that a tone of voice can mean much more than words. She learns that when she makes an excited noise, Grandma makes one, too; and she learns that when she is sad, Dad's sonorous singing can make it all better. She learns that she can make things happen with a point of her finger or a glance of her eye. She learns to solve problems and understand the world.

But what if your baby does not respond to the sound of your voice or learn to read the changes on your face? What if she doesn't play silly turn-taking games or does not grasp early on that her sounds and gestures have power? What if, for some reason, she does not master the first steps in that dance of learning and love?

A Missing Foundation

The child who, for whatever reason, is not attending to the social and emotional world around her is not learning all the things children learn by imitating and interacting with other people. So she is missing the foundations for basic social skills. But she also is missing the building blocks for broader learning. The long-term effects can be devastating. They go far beyond delayed speech or play skills. The child who is not connected socially and emotionally also may be falling behind in the development of language and complex, symbolic thinking and reasoning skills.

In other words, the baby who does not easily learn the first steps of human interaction—all those initial glances and smiles—does not easily learn the next steps either. Playing peekaboo may not seem like an intellectual building block, but it is. It teaches turn-taking, emotional regulation, conversational timing, and the principle of cause and effect, just to name a few things. Without such skills, children can't move on to real conversation and imaginative play and, from there, to higher-level abstract thinking. The older a child gets, the harder it is to teach her: not only is she missing basic skills but, quite likely, she's picked up lots of other behaviors that may interfere with learning. A child who should be soaking up knowledge every minute of the day may instead fill her hours with meaningless, self-absorbed rituals; the more deeply she sinks into her own world, the more unwilling she may be to join yours. Attempts to reach her may increasingly be met with fierce resistence. Meanwhile, that crucial early-learning window is closing.

"The mind and brain are growing very rapidly in the first three years of life and our most important human abilities are being mastered during that time," says the First Signs advising psychiatrist Dr Stanley I. Greenspan. "Children are learning complex social, emotional, intellectual, and language skills. If we allow a child to be off on the wrong pathway for a long period of time, we're doubling or tripling the ultimate challenges to that child."

For any parent who has even an inkling of concern about a child, it's important to understand this: what may seem like small, subtle differences in a baby or toddler can turn into much bigger differences later on. And when you see big differences in a very young child—when a four-month-old seems totally disconnected; when a one-year-old has absolutely no interest in people; when a two-year-old has figured out no way, verbal or nonverbal, to make a simple request for food or toys—you are seeing a child who could be in serious trouble. The problem may not be autism, but the child needs professional assessment right away.

The toddler who can't let you know what toy he wants turns into a grade-schooler who throws violent hour-long tantrums because he still has no better way to communicate; the baby who prefers shiny objects over human faces becomes a boy who can reprogram a computer but can't engage in the most simple everyday small talk. The child lacking basic social, emotional, and communication skills is at high risk for serious, lifelong disabilities—and the longer you wait to get help, the harder it is to help.

Early Help, Better Results

So, time is not on your side. But, if your child is very young, his developing brain is extremely adaptable. In the language of neuroscientists, it is "plastic." It can be molded much more easily than the brain of an older child or an adult. Remember, the wiring of the brain is not yet complete. New wires can still be laid down, sometimes bypassing faulty circuits; weak connections can be reinforced and become strong. Little problems can be corrected before they become big; even big problems can sometimes be eliminated or made small with the right kind of intensive, early therapy.

Although the particulars of various therapies and teaching methods vary greatly, they have one underlying assumption: the young brain is the most teachable brain. Children of all ages are still learning, of course, but an older brain just isn't biologically capable of making the rapid, strong connections that a younger brain can make. That's because the vast majority of brain cell connections, called synapses, form in those first three years; a more limited number continue to form up until age ten or so. After that, brain development is mostly a matter of pruning: an adult brain has only about half as many synapses as a three-year-old brain. It's also during the earliest years that active brain cells become coated with a fatty protective substance called myelin; the process of myelination, which appears critical for expanding brain function, occurs most rapidly during the first two years and then much more slowly through the rest of childhood and adolescence.

The brain also becomes increasingly specialized during early development. Some brain regions specialize in language, others in motor skills, still others in auditory perception, and so on. And these specialized areas get increasingly set in their ways as a child gets older. Early on, the brain can adapt, switching skills from one area to another, working around biological glitches, finding new pathways when the usual pathways are blocked. Later on, that all becomes more difficult.

Of course, early intervention can be hard work, too. But it's worth it, because it works. In recent years, some of the strongest evidence for the value of early intervention has come in the field of autism. Studies have shown that children with autism who receive intensive, early help enter their school years with higher IQs and less need for special education. Some (and no one yet knows how many) can make remarkable progress and learn to socialize, communicate, and think creatively, with none of the differences that would otherwise set them apart from their peers. It is possible for a toddler with severe social, emotional, and communication deficits to become as gregarious, talkative, playful, and loving as any typical child by the time she reaches grade school. Dr. Greenspan and some other leading researchers believe that, despite what some of the literature suggests, it is even possible for children on the autism spectrum to develop high-level abstract thinking skills and to learn to understand and empathize with other people—to develop "theory of mind," the ability to interpret the thoughts and feelings of others.

Of course, not all children with autism or related disorders do as well. But researchers say most make substantial progress when they get the right help early on. For some children, that might mean developing enough appropriate speech and social skills to function part or most of the time in a mainstream classroom—and later, to live and work independently or with minimal assistance. For others, it might mean developing much more rudimentary skills; a child with no speech might learn to communicate with pictures or sign language; another child with extremely disruptive, aggressive behavior might learn to behave appropriately at home and in public, dramatically improving the quality of life for an entire family.

Children with a broader range of developmental delays, disorders, and risk factors also reap clear benefits from early intervention. The best-studied group are children who come from poor families and have attended Head Start and similar preschool programs. These children often are at risk because of factors including poor nutrition and poor health care, coupled with a lack of enriching educational and social experiences. The studies show that, when compared to similar children who don't get early help, these children enter kindergarten better prepared. They have higher IQs, do better on standardized tests, and are less likely to need special education. There's some question about whether the intellectual benefits are permanent. But it is known that these children reach their teen years with fewer emotional and behavior problems than ers and are more likely to graduate from high school and os as young adults.

rt-term gains are even better documented. I hear again and again of children who begin to respond and learn within days or weeks of beginning an appropriate education and therapy program—one based on an accurate assessment of the child's developmental profile and targeted to his or her most urgent needs. Sarah said her first meaningful word within a week of starting speech therapy. The word? "Help." Nothing could state the case more clearly: children who are lagging in social, emotional, and communication skills need help. When they get it, their lives and the lives of their families improve almost immediately.

The Boston neurologist Margaret Bauman, a First Signs adviser, says one of her greatest joys is seeing a child who, with just a few months of intense intervention, suddenly is talking, playing, and interacting. You only need to see that kind of transformation once, she says, to know that early intervention is "really great stuff."

We saw instant changes in him. His tantrums went from about four a day to about four a week. And I could see early on, week to week, the connection he was making with his speech therapist. And I thought, "This is it, this is what he needs, this is how he can learn."

Susan Sutherland of Massachusetts, mother of Evan,
diagnosed with PDD-NOS just before age three

As soon as we started occupational and speech therapy, her language took off like wildfire. And by the end of her first year of preschool, she was just flying.

Penny Kelly of Connecticut, mother of Katie,
diagnosed with sensory integration
dysfunction at age two

Sometimes, progress is even more sudden. In her book *The Boy Who Loved Windows*, Patricia Stacey tells about a long, exhausting day she and her husband spent learning how to engage their son Walker through Floortime, a technique developed by Dr. Greenspan and his colleague the pyschologist Serena Wieder. Floortime, described in detail in Greenspan and Wieder's *The Child with Special Needs,* requires parents to relentlessly pursue real, meaningful back-and-forth communication with their child. During their training session, Dr. Greenspan stressed that Walker, just eleven months old and showing early signs of autism, had to be taught that communicating with his parents would make good things happen. At dinner that night at a nearby restaurant, Patricia tried one of his suggestions. She held up a cup and offered it to Walker if he would squeeze her finger. She writes: "The boy who had previously never responded to a verbal request put his hand up to mine and squeezed."

If Your Child Is Older

I want to stop here and address parents who may be concerned about a child who is older than three. Maybe your child's differences are so subtle that you have just begun to notice them. Maybe you've been concerned for a while, but, for one reason or another, have not sought help. Or you have sought help, and had your concerns dismissed. You may even be the parent of a child who has been misdiagnosed and improperly treated in the past.

It is not too late to help your child. While earlier help may be better, a child of four or five—or even ten, for that matter—still has a huge capacity for learning. Although brain development slows as a child passes through the preschool years, it does not stop. In fact, the most recent studies show that it continues throughout life and certainly goes through many important phases between toddlerhood and the teen years.

It is true that an older child is more set in his ways and may have established some hard-to-change behaviors that will get in the way of his learning. An older child who has not yet received appropriate therapy also may be much further behind his peers than a younger child with the same underlying deficits, whether those are in processing language, planning motor actions, regulating emotions, or tolerating sensations. Clearly, a child who has been having uncontrollable tantrums for seven or ten years is going to need more help than a two-year-old with the same problem. A five-year-old with limited language is going to face a much greater learning challenge than a twenty-month-old whose brain is near its language-learning peak. But many of the interventions that work for very young children can also work for older children, not only to correct disruptive behaviors but also to enhance learning, communication, social skills, and emotional competence. In general, progress will be slower. But each child is an individual and some children who begin appropriate therapy relatively late still do well. And, like younger children, almost all make some progress.

One boy was misdiagnosed with moderate mental retardation until he was four and a half. His mother said he seemed to be learning nothing in his special-needs preschool. Then he was correctly diagnosed with autism. After a few months of intensified speech and behavioral therapy, the boy's apparent IQ rose more than 25 points. After two years, he was reading, writing, and doing first-grade math.

Another woman, in Canada, who has a fifty-two-year-old brother with autism, told me recently that he had started "talking a blue streak" and had learned to write, thanks to some new computer training. Truly, it is never too late.

So, when it comes to helping your child, there's no such thing as "game over." Pick up the ball—and run.

Wait and See?

We know that intervention, especially early intervention, can change lives. We know that children learn best when they are very young and their brains are most plastic.

And yet, what three words do parents hear constantly when they express concern to a pediatrician or other professional? "Wait and see." It may happen to you. You may have a son who isn't talking and be told that "boys talk later than girls." You may have a with-drawn daughter and hear "She's just going through a phase." You may notice some unusual behavior, only to be told that your child is just "quirky."

You may even hear that most such problems disappear on their own. Yes, some less important problems—like trouble pronouncing certain sounds or performing certain fine motor tasks can improve over time and might not be urgent. But when a child is falling behind in crucial, core areas, when he isn't engaging in back-and-forth communication and isn't learning to understand the human world around him, that child needs immediate help. He needs a full evaluation "yesterday," says Dr. Greenspan. "You can't wait nine months. You can't even wait two months."

> My son didn't say "Mommy" or "Daddy." He didn't bab-
> ble. He didn't play with other kids. When we would take
> him to get a haircut he would have uncontrollable tantrums.
> So these were the kinds of things I would take to my pedia-
> trician. But she would dismiss them as "just his personality.
> He's doing things on his terms. He'll play with kids when he
> wants to. He'll speak when he wants to." She just wasn't
> concerned. Finally, she said at his two-year checkup: "I can
> see you're feeling strongly that something needs to be done.
> Let's look at him again in a few months and see."
>
> *Susan Sutherland of Massachusetts, mother of*
> *Evan, diagnosed with PDD-NOS*
> *just before age three*

Why do pediatricians let children wait? After all, doctors today are more knowledgeable than ever about autism and other disorders of communicating and relating. But many still don't know enough. Your doctor, for example, may not know that

- parent observations are highly reliable. When parents are anxious, there's a reason. While doctors may do a few parents a service by dismissing unwarranted concerns, they run the risk of overlooking children with real problems when they assume that worried parents are merely victims of an obsessive, hyperparenting culture.

• developmental disorders are not nearly as rare as once believed. In fact, their incidence seems to be growing.

• screening works. By asking a few questions and making a few observations, one can quickly sort out which children need the most immediate help. Waiting and watching a child with a low word count might be okay for a month or two; waiting and watching a child with a low word count, no gesturing, poor eye contact, and no play skills is not okay.

• early intervention works, in the short and long term. Doctors not familiar with the latest research may hold the now discredited belief that children with certain disorders—including autism and mental retardation—face a uniformly grim future, no matter what help they get.

• for worried parents, more information is better than less. When in doubt, doctors should refer children for further evaluation. If a child turns out to have a problem, that child and his family can get immediate help; if a child turns out to be fine, his relieved parents will be able to focus with greater confidence on his healthy development.

• help for young children with developmental delays is available in every community and—by law—many services are available at no cost to the family, or at a reduced cost.

The most important thing we've learned about autism in the last ten years is that early identification leads to the best outcomes. Anyone who tells you that children with autism can't get better doesn't really know much about autism.

Peter Bell of California, father of a boy with autism
and executive director of Cure Autism Now

There are other reasons your child's doctor might not respond to your concerns or might not raise his or her own concerns at the first available moment. One, of course, is that doctors always are pressed for time. They often get little or no additional payment from insurers for developmental screening. But there's also this: doctors are human. They don't like to give bad news. And they don't want to believe bad news. Sometimes, it's just easier to deny that a problem exists and to hope it will go away. Many went into pediatrics because they wanted a medical specialty focused on health rather than sickness. They chose a profession that relies on cordial, long-term relationships with parents. They don't want to risk alienating a parent by suggesting a developmental delay in a child who might show up six months later looking perfectly fine.

> I wanted to believe that nothing was wrong. My pediatrician suggested we see a specialist just to rule it out—I believe she said, "What do we have to lose?" In retrospect, I now understand just what we would have lost if we hadn't found out about my son's autism at age three. We would have lost valuable time; we would have wasted my son's potential. Now, after five years of special interventions, my son has made more progress than if we had waited.
>
> Julia O'Connor of New Hampshire, whose son
> Alexander received a provisional diagnosis of
> Asperger syndrome at age 3

Dealing with Your Own Denial

Perhaps you are the one who is putting off that frank discussion. Maybe you are the one in denial, disbelieving what seems too awful to face, wishing it away. I know the signs, because I've been there myself. I remember obsessively reading and rereading all of my baby books, knowing that my daughter was behind in some areas; I could see it every time I took her to Gymboree and observed other children her age. Yet I constantly talked myself out of my worries. Not that I named my fears out loud: to speak of them might make them real.

I found all sorts of ways to justify my daughter's differences. I convinced myself that Sarah didn't talk much because she was constantly around an overtalkative (though very loving) nanny. And I told myself that when she obsessively paced back and forth in her crib, it was "just a funny game." Meanwhile, I worked hard to compensate for her delays. Every time I changed her diaper, I tried to get her to play patty-cake; I tried not to worry when she just wasn't interested. When I noticed that Sarah would put shapes into a shape sorter in only one particular order—repeating the sequence, over and over again—I tried, in vain, to get her to do it another way. I knew there was something odd about this rigid behavior, but I just didn't want to think about it. I studied her every move, trying to anticipate her wants and needs—because, I know now, she was not effectively communicating them herself.

When doctors and others told me there was nothing to worry about, it was music to my ears: exactly what I wanted to hear. You may well hear the same, the first time you raise a concern. Before you accept the reassurance, though, ask yourself a few questions:

- Have you decided that your child is okay on the basis of good information? Have you checked your child's developmental progress in all areas, including specific social, emotional, and communication skills? Does your child's doctor use a formal screening tool?
- Are you constantly rationalizing or explaining away your child's differences? Guessing, for example, that your second child isn't talking because his big sister does all his talking for him? Musing, perhaps, that a withdrawn child is too caught up in his own big thoughts to bother with other people? Imagining genius in a child who loves books but ignores a classroom full of toys and potential playmates?

- Are you compensating for your child's differences? Are you, for example, adhering to rigid routines in order to prevent tantrums in an overly rigid child? Are you constantly guessing the needs of a child who's old enough to communicate them himself?
- Are other people—your spouse, your child's grandparents, preschool teachers, nannies, friends, neighbors—expressing worries about your child?

We knew he was hyperactive but we didn't pick up on any language problem. His preschool teacher immediately saw something was wrong. She brought it to my attention and said, "It could be ADHD, it could even be autism." Well, I just turned that idea off and I didn't want to hear it. But after a few months, we did have him evaluated. He was almost four and he tested at the level of an eighteen-month-old communication-wise. So we immediately put him in a special preschool program and he's done really well since then.

Rhonda Twitty of South Carolina, mother of Daniel,
diagnosed with language delays and ADHD

A special word about spouses: when one parent is worried about a child and another is not, denial often wins out, a least for a while. After all, who wants to get into this kind of argument with a husband or wife? Who wants to be the one to insist that something is wrong with your beautiful, precious child? Or to schedule a costly doctor appointment that your spouse thinks is a waste of money? The best advice I can give you, if you are the worried parent, is to follow your gut. Get all the information you need to either confirm or rule out a problem. Then you and your spouse can make decisions about your child based on those facts.

In the beginning when my husband even mentioned autism, I was very insulted. "My son's not autistic. Are you crazy? I'm not putting him with kids like that." I really didn't believe it. . . . But if I had a doctor say to me, "You know, I'm a little concerned. Why don't we go and check this avenue out," I think I would have listened more.

Sharon Oberleitner of Idaho, mother of Robby,
diagnosed with autism at age three

Like spouses, other relatives and friends can be on either side of the denial fence. Sometimes, grandparents, with all their experience, are among the first to notice a problem and raise a concern. And sometimes—because they love their grandchildren so much and are suspicious of what they may see as a trend toward overanxious parenting—they are the last to acknowledge that something's amiss. Friends can also work to support or break through your denial. Some may feel it is their job to lessen any worries you have, to regale you with stories of late-talking Harvard grads and their own wonderfully eccentric, yet perfectly typical children. That kind of talk is fun—when your own child is perfectly typical, too. When your heart is telling you that that is not the case, it only increases your uncertainty. It can also make you feel very alone.

People kept telling me, "You're overprotective, you're worrying too much, you're a typical first-time parent."

Karin Cather of Virginia, mother of two boys
diagnosed with autism spectrum disorders

Other friends may speak up and express a concern about your child. It may be a passing comment on a playground: "Gosh, it doesn't seem like Ryan is hearing you. Do you think his hearing is okay?" Or it could be a blunt call for action. "He's still not talking? If he were mine, I'd take him to the doctor tomorrow."

In my own case, it was a worried grandmother—and a whole lot of indisputable facts—that finally broke through my denial about Sarah. As a result, I got my daughter the help she needed, help that made all the difference because it came during the crucial early years.

If you are concerned about a child—of any age—today is the day to start finding out what that child needs. Time *does* matter. I can't supply a concerned grandmother to increase your sense of urgency. But I can give you more facts. Once you have those facts about what's really essential in a child's social and emotional development you will know the next, best steps for your child.

To Do Now

Here's one thing you can do right now to make the most of your child's early years: turn off the TV.

Whether your child is developing typically or has some delays, TV has absolutely no value for children under age two. The American Academy of Pediatrics says infants and toddlers should watch no TV. That means no *Barney,* no *Teletubbies,* and no "Baby Einstein" videos. Despite the marketing claims, these shows and videos are highly unlikely to enhance development in a very young child and may distract him from more valuable learning experiences.

For children over age two, the academy recommends no more than one to two hours a day of carefully chosen TV, videos, and computer games. And many professionals who work with children who have developmental delays urge parents to limit "screen time" even more, and to think of it as a break for themselves rather than a learning experience for their children.

Also, remember this: a child might learn some language from TV and videos, but she's much more likely to learn words—and their social meaning—when you talk, read, and sing with her.

~ Luke's Story

Kathie and Carl Tomczuk were conscientious parents. So when their son Luke showed signs of muscle weakness and he wasn't walking by sixteen months, they made an appointment with a physical therapist. By the time they got to the appointment a few weeks later, Luke was walking. So the therapist asked about Luke's other skills. Only then did they realize that their son, who had used some words around twelve months, well before his twin sister, had stopped talking.

Soon, his parents noticed other things—such as the fact that Luke often failed to respond when they called his name. And often, instead of playing with his sister or older brother, Luke paced around their Philadelphia house and flapped his hands. Or he sat alone for hours, engrossed in the noisy, flashing electronic toys he loved.

At his eighteen-month checkup, Luke's pediatrician agreed that there was reason for concern and referred the family to a developmental pediatrician. Finally, at age two, Luke got his first diagnosis: global developmental delays. But his parents had no idea what that meant, beyond the fact that Luke was not meeting a lot of milestones. Six months later, the developmental pediatrician was blunt: she thought Luke had "moderate mental retardation." He wasn't talking, she said, because he had "nothing to say." The Tomczuks were devastated. But on her report that day, the doctor also wrote "pervasive developmental disorder—not otherwise specified"—saying that the label probably wasn't accurate but might help Luke get more services. She didn't explain what "PDD-NOS" meant.

Kathie, who was studying to become a teacher, went home, got on the Internet, and looked it up. "I said, 'Oh, my God, he has autism.' I knew right away." And she knew the doctor must have known it six months earlier. "In a phone call shortly after that, she told me parents can't handle the autism diagnosis and need to be eased into it. That ridiculous judgment call on her part cost us months of progress."

Angry but energized, Kathie went into mission mode. She scoured the Internet and bought an armful of books. She found stories of children with autism who were severely retarded and never learned to talk or function independently in any way. And she was frightened. But she also found stories of hope and learned that some children with autism made amazing progress.

And at about that time, Luke himself spoke up, in his own way. One day, Kathie walked into the playroom where Luke was playing alone and found his name scrawled on a chalkboard. Kathie's heart leapt at the sight, but she couldn't believe her eyes. So she erased the name, left the room, and, a few minutes later, returned. He'd written it again. Her two-year-old son, declared mute by an expert doctor, did have something to say, after all. "I knew he was in there," Kathie says.

Determined to reach the boy inside, the Tomczuks enrolled Luke in an intense therapy called applied behavioral analysis (ABA). Every day, therapists came to the family's house and worked with Luke, teaching him, though constant repetition and reward, the things that other children learn automatically, such as paying attention to people and responding to their voices and gestures. Luke started with just six hours of ABA a week, but eventually—after his parents convinced their local Early Intervention program to pay for the costly sessions—he was in therapy forty hours a week. It became his full-time job.

And the work paid off. At first, Luke responded—following simple directions, imitating actions, sounds, and words, and taking the first steps toward real communication—only when he was working with a therapist. Slowly, though, he began to interact with his family. After a while, his big brother and twin sister began to come to many of the sessions, so they all could learn to talk and play together.

When Luke was four, his parents tackled another problem. Luke, always a picky eater, had slowly reduced the list of foods he would eat to just peanut butter and Ritz crackers. Desperate, Kathie and Carl enrolled him in a hospital program where he would be trained to accept a greater variety of foods. At the same time, they made another decision: they would introduce only foods free of casein (a protein in milk) and gluten (found in wheat and other grains). The Tomczuks had read that some children with autism seem to feel better, and to learn and develop faster, while on a gluten- and casein-free diet. They had no idea if it would help Luke. But they didn't want to regret not trying it. After the diet switch, Luke seemed healthier, stronger, and more coordinated; his speech even seemed more understandable. So his parents kept it up.

By then, Luke was doing so well that his parents saw no reason that he could not start preschool—in a regular classroom—along with his twin sister. So Kathie was shocked when teachers and administrators at the first two preschools she visited discouraged her from enrolling him. One actually handed her a contract that said the school did not accept children who were "handicapped or retarded." By the time she got to a third preschool, she decided not to mention that her son had autism. She said only that he had speech delays and would need the help of an aide (supplied by the family). Luke was accepted, attended the school for two years, and thrived there. Eventually, Kathie told the school's director about Luke's diagnosis. But, she says, "I'm sure they figured it out when we came in wearing our 'Cure Autism Now' T-shirts."

Meanwhile, Luke kept up the home ABA, plus speech and

occupational therapies and his special diet. All of it seemed to help. At age six, he went off to kindergarten at the same school his sister had started a year earlier. And, with just an aide in the classroom to help him along, he did just fine.

Today, Luke is eight, part of a regular second grade and getting good grades. He still has an aide in his classroom, but her help is minimal: "She'll be standing across the room and clear her throat if she sees him staring out the window," Kathie says.

Luke still paces sometimes at home. He's a bit awkward with other kids and often doesn't know how to strike up or maintain a conversation. Instead, he spins out monologues about geography, presidents, highways, and train routes. With adults and family members, he does much better—engaging in good conversations about all sorts of things, especially sports. And recently, he joined a baseball team, his first not just for kids with disabilities. His mom was nervous, but cheered as he hit two singles in his first game.

"He's not recovered. There are still issues. But he's almost as recovered as you can get without making it over that hump," Kathie says. She has no doubt that Luke's relatively early diagnosis and intense treatment made the difference. Luke himself tells people that he "used to have autism." Recently, he asked Kathie to "look in his head and see if there is any autism there." And he said he would like to "invent a machine to change the past and make all the autism go away for everybody."

The conversations are getting complicated, Kathie says. "The fact that Luke and I can even have this discussion is amazing. He is amazing."

Chapter Three
Developmental Milestones and Sharing Concerns

Imagine a waiting room full of babies—a busy pediatrics office, say. Now, imagine you have the power to see into the future. Look closely at the babies now. In one corner, you see an active little guy named Max. You see that Max will be walking at ten months, saying his first word—"No"—at fourteen months, and dressing himself by age two. Now take a look at Emily, the sleeping baby next to Max. You see that Emily will say "Mama," "Dada," "hi," and "doggie," all before her first birthday, will take her first steps at sixteen months, and will still be tangling herself in her T-shirts at age three. Then, there's baby James. He's the one wailing his heart out. You see that he'll be walking at twelve months, saying his first word—"shoe"—at thirteen months, and dressing himself, shoes and all, by age three.

Which of these children is developing in a healthy way? It's quite possible that all of them are—or that none of them are. Certainly Max, Emily, and James are developing lots of important skills and acquiring them at a pace that is well within the ranges usually seen in typical children. And there's no reason to worry about Emily walking a little later than Max, or about James talking a little later than Emily. Every child is unique and so is his or her exact developmental path.

But to know whether Max, Emily, or James is at risk for a developmental disorder—especially for a disorder of relating or communicating—we'd have to know a lot more about them. We'd have to know if they are just learning to talk—or really learning to communicate. We'd have to know if they are just learning to walk—or are also learning to master the intricate dance of social and emotional connection.

The Milestones of Development

Many books about baby and child development include lists of milestones, those things that children typically do at certain ages (for example, "Walks independently at age 12–15 months"). The best of these books—and there are several very good ones—make the point that the milestones are general guideposts to typical development. So the mother of a four-month-old can read that most babies that age can lift their heads up 90 degrees, but that a baby who doesn't spend much time on his tummy might do that a little later. And the father of a twenty-one-month-old can read that his child probably should be climbing stairs, but that he shouldn't worry too much if his "late bloomer" isn't quite there.

Likewise, most physicians and nurse practitioners will ask about some milestones during well-child visits. They'll certainly ask about motor skills: Is your five-month-old rolling over? Is your seven-month-old sitting up? And they may ask about apparent cognitive development: Can your nine-month-old find a hidden toy? Can your three-year-old count three objects?

Such milestones are important, and falling behind can mean that your child is in developmental trouble. If you find that your child is not meeting milestones mentioned in other books or emphasized by your health care provider, you should have her screened for developmental delays. A delay in large motor skills, such as rolling over or sitting up, for instance, could reflect an individual difference, or it could be a sign of an underlying problem ranging from cerebral palsy to mental retardation to a heart defect. A delay could be temporary—the result of premature birth or of an illness—or it could have long-lasting consequences. In any case, you need to check it out.

But this is what I want you to know: the milestones emphasized in most books and by most health care providers don't tell the complete story. That's because they don't focus enough on key social, emotional, and communication skills. So a child lagging behind on motor skills might be missing even more critical social skills, yet get assessment and help only for the motor skills. And a child meeting all those common motor and cognitive milestones could nevertheless have a problem, and get no early help at all. That ten-month-old walker or sixteen-month-old stair-climber could have a serious communication difficulty. Even a child who appears highly intelligent—the toddler who can always find where you've hidden the cookies; the two-year-old who is starting to read—could be falling behind in ways that could severely limit her long-term development.

Even if the child is keeping up with the word counts in all the toddler development books, you still can't be sure about her unless you know the difference between words and meaningful communication. One child knew twenty-six words at the age of eighteen months, a fine vocabulary by the standards of most developmental milestone charts. The problem? All twenty-six words were the letters of the alphabet, which the child enjoyed saying to himself, over and over again. He was talking, but he certainly wasn't communicating.

> He spoke early. He had lots and lots of words. By a year
> he had fifty words. . . . But it wasn't conversational language.
> He was just doing a lot of labeling.
>
> *Beth Corcoran, mother of Joey, diagnosed with an*
> *autism spectrum disorder at thirty months*

A Different Kind of Development

It is very important to follow your child's social and emotional development and to track his communication skills, no matter how many other milestones he is meeting. The question is, Just what should you watch for?

Luckily, we know much more about that than we did just a few years ago. Much of this knowledge comes from detailed observational studies of healthy, typical babies and toddlers. Increasingly, researchers also are collecting solid information about children who have developmental delays. In the past, they mostly relied on parents' memories of babies and toddlers who were later diagnosed with certain disorders. More recently, they have started asking these parents for videotapes of their children's early months. Watching these tapes, the researchers have learned to recognize the subtle signs of social delay and disconnection, signs that parents and pediatricians often miss. In one famous study, researchers looked at first-birthday-party tapes of children later diagnosed with autism: the children showed specific delays in social and communication skills that experts now recognize as early signs of the disorder.

These days researchers are taking their studies a step further: they are directly monitoring high-risk babies and toddlers (including younger siblings of children with autism) and then following them for months and years to see how their social and emotional development plays out and how it sometimes goes astray.

Using clues gathered from these studies, the best-informed professionals are now identifying and helping some children with social, emotional, and communication delays before their first birthdays. And the experts say that almost any child with a disorder of relating or communicating can be recognized before reaching the age of two. These are children who, in the past, would not have been diagnosed or treated until age three or much later.

There's no reason your child can't get the same kind of early help if he or she needs it. You just need to know what these researchers know: what healthy development looks like. Children who are developing in a healthy way are, from a very early age:

- paying a lot of attention to the voices, faces, and actions of other people
- showing a lot of pleasure in other people
- engaging in back-and-forth communication—both verbal and nonverbal

With practice and a little more information, you'll learn to recognize this kind of healthy development. It's the four-month-old, sitting in her bouncy seat, watching your face as you talk. You smile at her, and she smiles right back. Just a few months later, that same baby can hold a kind of conversation: you speak to her and she babbles back at you; you take a turn and then she takes a turn; you walk away and she screeches to make you come back. And then she's a one-year-old, taking you by the hand to the playroom; you get there and she points to the top of a shelf. "Do you want Elmo?" you ask, and she nods and says, "Elmo!," pointing and laughing as you raise her up to reach for the toy. She's the two-year-old looking at you seriously and saying "Shhhhh" as she puts her doll to sleep. She's the three-year-old holding hands, laughing, and whispering with her best preschool friend.

The researchers who have put together this picture of healthy social development say it is more than a matter of discrete milestones: it is a complete picture, a *package* of skills and behaviors that children need in order to be effective communicators, learners, and members of the social world. It's not just making eye contact—it's being able to read the meaning in other people's faces. It's not just smiling and laughing—it's smiling and laughing in response to the funny things other people do and say. It's not just using and understanding words—it's using and understanding words and, just as important, gestures and facial expressions, to exchange information and emotions with other people. And finally, it's the ability to put all those individual skills together in a smooth, purposeful stream of rich social engagement.

A Different Kind of Milestone List

Just as you can't predict a child's future athletic prowess by knowing when he first sat up, you can't predict a child's future social prowess by knowing when she first smiled at you. It's the bigger picture that counts. But milestones still matter. One important goal at First Signs has been to put together a checklist of specific social, emotional, and communication milestones, which you can use as a general barometer of your child's development. The result is the First Signs Developmental Milestones Checklist ("Is Your Baby Meeting These Important Milestones?"), a collaborative effort based on the research and writings of three top experts in child development: Dr. Stanley I. Greenspan and the speech and language experts Barry M. Prizant and Amy M. Wetherby.

As you look through the list, you'll see that it elaborates on the principles mentioned earlier. Healthy children are attending to and engaging with the people around them with real joy, and they are able to engage in back-and-forth communication, known as social reciprocity, from a very early age. The expected skills are relatively simple at younger ages and more complex later on. One skill builds upon another. The child who is not exchanging smiles at four months may not be exchanging words at fifteen months. The child who masters games like patty-cake and peekaboo at twelve months is on the road to more complex, pretend play at thirty-six months.

First, look over the list and find your child's age. Is he doing everything listed? Did he achieve the milestones listed for earlier ages on time—and if not, has he caught up now? Has she lost any milestone skills that she had in the past? As in applying any milestone list, you should make adjustments if your child was born prematurely (for example, if he was two months early, expect him to show the listed skills about two months later than other children, at least up until age two or so).

Maybe you'll notice that your child is consistently stronger in some areas than in others. For example, some children seem notably better at communicating through gestures than through sounds, while others show the opposite pattern. Still others seem much better at understanding speech than at producing it themselves. And some, including many children at risk for autism spectrum disorders, will show a marked weakness in using and understanding both sounds and gestures. Make a note of any pattern. Eventually it could help you to put together a profile of your child's strengths and weaknesses.

Also, keep in mind that these are skills involved in relationships. Children may be much more likely to demonstrate them with parents and other caregivers than with unfamiliar people, including doctors. So, once again, as a parent you have a unique ability to follow this kind of development in your child and to share your findings with others.

Still, you may feel unsure about whether your child is meeting some of these milestones. You may never have thought about how many gestures your child uses or whether he can keep up a long stream of back-and-forth babbling. Like most parents, you may be so busy with day-to-day demands—including caring for other children, managing the household, holding down a job—that you have not yet tuned in to some of your child's subtle behaviors or differences. So, as you go through the list, check off any skills you may need to test—and then test them. If you aren't sure whether your one-year-old consistently responds to his name, spend a day gathering data. Call to him from across the room and then from another room; try it again at the dinner table, at the playground, and during a quiet story time. And if the skill is inconsistent—if he responds in quiet settings but not loud ones, or responds only one out of four times—make a note of that.

Also, consider the quality of your child's skills: that is, don't be satisfied that your eighteen-month-old is meeting the vocabulary milestone for (ten words) unless you are quite certain that he understands the words and is using them for communication on a regular basis. It's one thing to say "Cheese" when you want a cube of mozzarella or you're having your picture taken. It's quite another to say "Cheese" over and over, all day—as my daughter did—when there are no dairy products or cameras in sight.

Is Your Baby Meeting These Important Milestones?

Key Social, Emotional, and Communication Milestones for Your Baby's Healthy Development

Does Your Baby . . .

At 4 Months:
- ❑ Follow and react to bright colors, movement, and objects?
- ❑ Turn toward sounds?
- ❑ Show interest in watching people's faces?
- ❑ Smile back when you smile?

At 6 Months:
- ❑ Relate to you with real joy?
- ❑ Smile often while playing with you?
- ❑ Coo or babble when happy?
- ❑ Cry when unhappy?

At 9 Months:
- ❑ Smile and laugh while looking at you?
- ❑ Exchange back-and-forth smiles, loving faces, and other expressions with you?
- ❑ Exchange back-and-forth sounds with you?
- ❑ Exchange back-and-forth gestures with you, such as giving, taking, and reaching?

At 12 Months:

❏ Use a few gestures, one after another, to get needs met, like giving, showing, reaching, waving, and pointing?

❏ Play peekaboo, patty-cake, or other social games?

❏ Make sounds, like "ma," "ba," "na," "da," and "ga"?

❏ Turn to the person speaking when his or her name is called?

At 15 Months:

❏ Exchange with you many back-and-forth smiles, sounds, and gestures in a row?

❏ Use pointing or other "showing" gestures to draw attention to something of interest?

❏ Use different sounds to get needs met and draw attention to something of interest?

❏ Use and understand at least three words, such as "mama," "dada," "bottle," or "bye-bye"?

At 18 Months:

❏ Use lots of gestures with words to get needs met, such as pointing or taking you by the hand and saying, "Want juice"?

❏ Use at least four different consonants (for instance, "m," "n," "p," "b," "t," "d") in babbling or in words?

❏ Use and understand at least ten words?

❏ Show that he or she knows the names of familiar people or body parts by pointing to them or looking at them when they are named?

❏ Do simple pretend play, like feeding a doll or stuffed animal and attracting your attention by looking up at you?

At 24 Months:

❏ Do pretend play with you with more than one action, like feeding the doll and then putting the doll to sleep?

❏ Use and understand at least fifty words?

❏ Use at least two words together (without imitating or repeating) and in a way that makes sense, like "Want juice"?

❑ Enjoy being next to children of the same age and show interest in playing with them, perhaps giving a toy to another child?

❑ Look for familiar objects out of sight when asked?

At 36 Months:

❑ Enjoy pretending to play different characters with you or talking "for" dolls or action figures?

❑ Enjoy playing with children of the same age, perhaps showing and telling another child about a favorite toy?

❑ Use thoughts and actions together in speech and in play in a way that makes sense, like "Sleepy, go take nap" and "Baby hungry, feed bottle"?

❑ Answer "what," "where," and "who" questions easily?

❑ Talk about interests, and about feelings about the past and the future?

Encouraging Social Communication

You can try a few techniques, called communicative temptations, to help draw out appropriate responses in a child between the ages of nine and fifteen months. These communicative temptations were developed by Wetherby and Prizant as part of a clinical assessment procedure (see *Communication and Symbolic Behavior Scales Developmental Profile* in Resources). Here are a few you can try:

• Point to an object and say "Look" to your child. Does she look?

• Blow bubbles. Does she react with smiles and joy?

• Then put the same closed jar of bubbles in front of your child. Does she signal for help to open the jar?

• Start up a wind-up toy and let it stop in front of the child. Does she react? Does she signal for help to wind it up again?

It's important to understand that your child does not have to use words to communicate in any of these situations. The key is that she should be fixing her eyes on yours, trying to gain your attention, and trying intently—using every skill at her disposal—to communicate her desires and needs to you. That may mean grinning at you gleefully as the bubbles float over her head or pounding the table and glancing at you when the wind-up toy stops. It could mean looking at you expectantly when you put that closed bubble jar in front of her—and then patting the jar and grunting when you fail to act on her first cue.

Talk to Your Child's Doctor

If your child has achieved all the milestones on the chart and easily responds to all the communicative temptations, you should feel some assurance about your child's social, emotional, and communication development. However, you should not mistake the list for a formal screening that rules out any sort of problem. Likewise, if your child is missing some milestones, or if you still aren't sure about the quality and consistency of some important skills, you may have cause for concern. But you should not leap to conclusions and decide your child has any specific disorder.

What you should do—no matter how many of the milestones your child is achieving—is share your findings and any uneasiness you feel with a professional. Usually that means the pediatrician or family physician who sees your child for routine well-child care. Take a copy of the milestones chart to every well-child visit and use it to open a dialogue about healthy social and emotional development. Even if you think your child is doing fine, let your doctor know that you are interested in your child's total development and want it to be evaluated formally at every well-child visit.

Be clear: tell the doctor that you want her to do more than eyeball your child. You want her to help you figure out whether your child really is achieving the kinds of skills listed on this chart. And you want your doctor to perform her own formal screening test—one that is proven to identify children at risk for disorders of communicating and relating. And, if there's any cause for concern, you want your child to get a more wide-ranging, formal evaluation right away.

You can do your part by thoroughly preparing for your child's appointments:

- For each well-child visit at the ages of four, six, nine, twelve, fifteen, eighteen, twenty-four, and thirty-six months, copy, fill out, and bring the First Signs Developmental Milestones Checklist.
- Also note your child's progress with respect to the milestones (motor, cognitive, vision, hearing, and so on) that are described in other leading books. (I recommend *Building Healthy Minds,* by Stanley I. Greenspan; the "What to Expect" series; the *"Touchpoints"* books, by T. Berry Brazelton; and the classic books by Penelope Leach.)
- Keep a special notebook to record your questions and concerns in advance and to write down the doctor's responses. Be sure to include details about any behavior of your child's that seems unusual.
- Provide the front office staff with a separate written list of your questions when you check in. Ask them to have the physician review your questions before the exam. This will allow the doctor to be prepared and to use the allotted time to best effect.
- Keep and bring a record of your baby or toddler's height, weight, and head circumference, as measured in previous visits. Also keep and bring a vaccination record. Physicians should provide forms for these purposes that they can update for you at each visit. If you notice either unusual growth spurts or delays in any physical measurement, particularly head circumference, ask your clinician to review

this further. (Studies suggest that some children with autism have an unusual pattern of rapid early head growth. Slow head growth can also be cause for concern.)

- If your child's physician usually asks you to fill out a developmental screening questionnaire in the waiting room, prepare a bag with your child's favorite toys to keep him happy while you complete the forms.
- If your physician's practice has not had you fill out a developmental screening questionnaire in the past, call before your next visit and ask if and when they do screen. If they do not, you might suggest that a doctor or other staff member visit the First Signs website at www.first signs.org to find high-quality tools that work in busy practices. Or go to the website yourself, download a screening form, and bring it with you next time.

After thoroughly discussing the milestones chart and taking the other steps above, you may still have concerns about your child. If those concerns persist even after a physician or other professional says they are unwarranted, you have every right to pursue a formal evaluation for your child.

> We first noticed that Christopher was not developing speech. Up until about a year, he had met all his milestones, and it seemed like he was okay except his language wasn't coming. We compared him to other children and they had five words, they had six—and Chris didn't have any. As time went on, they were putting words together and still Chris was not developing language. So we went to a doctor and voiced our concerns, and he said not to worry about it, that he was a boy and boys usually develop speech later.
>
> *Ellen Weitzen of New Jersey, mother of Chris,*
> *diagnosed with autism at age three*

Red Flags

In some cases, a formal evaluation is absolutely essential and urgent. If your child is showing any "Red Flags," you should not wait for your next well-child visit to get help and you should not take no or "Wait and see" for an answer. Your child needs a full-scale developmental evaluation to either rule out serious problems—or to start the process of diagnosis and early intervention.

These are the Red Flags:

- no big smiles or other warm, joyful expressions by six months or thereafter
- no back-and-forth sharing of sounds, smiles, or other facial expressions by nine months or thereafter
- no babbling by twelve months
- no back-and-forth gestures, such as pointing, showing, reaching, or waving, by twelve months
- no words by sixteen months
- no two-word meaningful phrases (without imitating or repeating) by twenty-four months
- any loss of speech or babbling, or of social skills, at any age

Lucas developed fine at first. He sat on time, crawled, babbled, said hi, at seven months. Other moms talked about how advanced he was. But then around fifteen months he started a subtle regression. I was not really realizing it, though I was counting words he'd lost. I just thought he was going through a phase.

Mary Barbera of Pennsylvania, mother of Lucas,
diagnosed with autism at age three

Studies have demonstrated that these Red Flags are strongly linked to disorders of relating and communicating, especially to autism spectrum disorders. However, that your child shows one or more of them does not mean she has autism or any other disorder: It does mean that her developmental differences need to be checked out formally—and explained in some way—without further delay.

Research by Wetherby and her colleague Julian Woods at Florida State University suggests some other possible warning signs for autism spectrum disorders in the second year of life. They include:

- repetitive movements with objects (for example, flicking light switches on and off or making the same movement, with the same toy, over and over again)
- lack of appropriate eye gaze (the child has poor eye contact and also fails to follow the gazes of others, to see what they are looking at)
- lack of response to name (the child doesn't look at you or react in any way when you call his name)

> We thought Chris was completely deaf for a while. We would stand behind him and scream his name at the top of our lungs and he wouldn't budge.
>
> *Gary Weitzen of New Jersey, father of Chris,*
> *diagnosed with autism at age three*

Again, these signs do not necessarily mean that your child has autism or any developmental disorder. But they are reasons for concern and for further professional evaluation.

Even if you see these Red Flags, or find gaps in your child's milestone progress, you may remain reluctant to seek help. You may, especially, cling to certain myths. For example, you might think your child can't be in trouble if he or she generally is happy or affectionate toward you. This just is not true: happy, affectionate children may nevertheless be severely limited in their social and communication skills. It's also very common for parents to cling to signs that their child is intelligent, and to dismiss signs that the child may be limited in some other way. This is especially common when children have autism spectrum disorders, because many such children have what the experts call "splinter skills." That is, they can be very good at some things—perhaps reading or rote memorization of facts—but have significant delays in other areas. If you are the parent of a girl, you may cling to a belief that only boys have these problems. Autism and most other developmental disorders are more common in boys, but girls are diagnosed with these disorders every day. You may believe that only older children can be reliably diagnosed, or that treatment really won't help. None of these things is true.

> My son was two. I did not know what autism was all about. I had no personal experience with any disability or even typical child development. He was just this smart little boy who knew so many things that others didn't. It took me almost six months to really believe that he did have a disability, not just something temporary that would fix itself.
>
> *Joy Johnson of Maryland, mother of*
> *two boys with autism*

So look for the milestones. Look for the Red Flags. And, if there is cause for immediate concern, talk to your child's doctor right away.

Sharing Your Concerns

It's easy for me to urge you to share your concerns with professionals: I've been doing that on behalf of my daughter for many years now. But for you, this may be new, scary territory. Despite having some solid information now about worrisome developmental signs, you may not want to believe your eyes when you see those signs in your child. And you may still expect that a highly trained doctor will automatically recognize and act on a serious developmental problem. Sadly, that's often not the case. So, once again, you need to do your part to get your child the care he deserves.

Parent to Parent

Sometimes the first person to become concerned about a child's development is not a parent; it's a grandmother, a friend, a teacher, or a nanny. If you are concerned about a child who is not your own, you are in a tough spot. You want to help, but you don't want to alarm or offend the child's parents. The easiest thing might be to wait and hope that the parents eventually see what you see.

But, please, don't wait. While expressing your concerns may be uncomfortable at first, it's the right thing to do. It could help a child at risk get early, appropriate treatment. And you may be surprised: that mother or father you think is in the dark may be eager to talk about his or her own worries—worries that they may have been unable or unwilling to express up until now.

A few tips:

- Set the stage for a successful conversation. A quiet walk or coffee date might be better than a hurried chat in the preschool parking lot or a discussion in front of twenty relatives at Thanksgiving dinner.
- Start by asking the parent about his or her own observations, questions, or concerns. You might ask: "How's Tommy doing? Do you like your pediatrician? Do you talk about development?" Then you could mention that you've been reading about the importance of social, emotional, and communication development. Talk about some of the milestones—like whether the child is babbling or using gestures appropriately—and ask, "How is it going in those areas?"
- Respond with your own concerns. You might say: "Please understand that this is hard for me to bring up, but I care about you and Tommy so much that I just can't keep my concerns to myself. I've noticed some things that worry me. [Name some

specific behaviors or missing milestones.] Have you noticed these things, too? I'd like to help if I can."

- Focus on milestones, Red Flags, and the need to "rule out" anything serious. Share the checklist or talk about it in detail. Let parents know that physicians don't always check for these signs.
- Don't use labels, technical jargon, or loaded terminology. You won't help by saying, "I think your child is autistic" (or "retarded," or "cognitively impaired").
- Don't compare one child with another. That can put a parent on the defensive. The important thing isn't how a child compares to his cousins or playmates; it's whether his own developmental path is a healthy one.
- Suggest other resources. Some parents need to discover information on their own and come to their own understanding. A good starting point for anyone: www.firstsigns.org.
- Emphasize the importance of early identification and intervention. Say: "I'm sure you've heard all the talk about the importance of the first three years. Did you know that there are programs to help children if they fall behind and get them back on track while they're still little? You can even get a free evaluation."
- Put yourself in the parent's shoes. Be supportive, not judgmental. If a parent sees no cause for concern, say: "I'm glad you feel it's all going well. Please know I will always be here if you should ever have a concern or need an ear."

You can do it. Here's how.

- Be prepared. Take all of the steps outlined here before your child's next office visit. Don't forget to bring the milestones checklist and your own list of specific questions and concerns. If your doctor doesn't do routine screening, bring your own screening form, downloaded from the First Signs website at www.firstsigns.org.

- Express your concerns clearly and factually. Start by saying that you are concerned about your child's development and then give concrete examples; such as "My child doesn't respond to my voice," or "He spends so much time lining up toys, he has no interest in other children," or "She hasn't learned a new word in months," or "He doesn't look at me—he never makes eye contact." While you may feel very upset about these things, try to convey them in a calm manner. Again, it will help to write down the specifics in advance.

- Ask questions. The only dumb question is one you don't ask. If the doctor uses terms you don't understand, ask for an explanation. After any developmental screening, ask what the results are and what they mean. And if you don't get appropriate screening, be persistent and ask why. Remember, "Don't worry" and "Wait and see" are not acceptable responses.

- Listen carefully to the answers you get. One way to make sure you understand what a doctor has just told you is to repeat it. You can say something like "If I understand you correctly, you think he has a speech delay but is otherwise on track."

- Follow up. If your concerns are not adequately addressed in a routine appointment, ask for an immediate follow-up appointment. Return, preferably within a week or so, with even more documentation of your child's specific delays. If it's clear your child's doctor won't pursue your concerns, ask for a referral to a developmental pediatrician. And if your doctor does perform a screening and confirm your concerns, be sure to ask, "What's the next step?" You should get a referral to your community's Early Intervention program or school system. Depending on the nature of your child's problems, you may also want to pursue referrals to a developmental pediatrician, psychologist, neurologist, psychiatrist, or other professional experienced in diagnosing and treating children with autism and other developmental disorders.

Whatever you do, don't keep your concerns to yourself and don't be convinced that it is okay to wait and see. There is no downside to taking action.

I can happily attest that I sometimes get a follow-up call or e-mail from a parent who saw worrisome signs in a baby or toddler—but then saw the child get quickly back on track. One such parent, a woman in California, first contacted me when her son was eight months old. She was worried because he didn't smile or laugh much and sometimes ignored her when she called his name. I suggested that she speak with her pediatrician and, meanwhile, get a copy of *The Child with Special Needs* and try some of Dr. Greenspan's Floortime techniques. These techniques involve playing with a child in a way that will help him connect emotionally and engage in back-and-forth communication, first with gestures and expressions and then with words. This mom went right out, got the book, and put the techniques to work—and within a couple of months she was no longer concerned about her son. If anything, she said, he was more advanced and more social than the other kids around him—talking, singing, and playing up a storm with both his parents and with other kids. Was it the Floortime? Or just time? This parent will never know, but she told me she was tremendously relieved that there was something she could do to help her son—that she did not just have to "wait and see."

To Do Now

Go to the videotape. If you have trouble remembering what your child did at certain ages, get out your old videotapes and take a look. Pay special attention to key social, emotional, and communication skills. Did your baby babble a few months ago? Did your toddler point or wave? Do you see signs of disconnection that you missed at the time?

You can also use videotape to document your child's progress or lack of it. As you go through the milestones list and "communicative temptations" in this chapter, tape your attempts to engage your child. Brief snippets of these sessions could later help professionals understand your concerns.

Videotape is also a good way to document worrisome behaviors, such as repetitive, obsessive play, or unusual movements that could be seizures or tics.

Part Two
The Path to Diagnosis

You've watched your child grow and develop and, for one reason or another, you've had concerns. Maybe, after reading about key milestones and Red Flags, you are quite worried. You may even be convinced that your child has a disorder.

Now what? Your instinct may be to start researching whatever disorder you suspect, or to run straight to your pediatrician's office and demand that he or she diagnose your child on the spot. After all, answers are urgently needed.

But I want you to find the *best* answers for your child. That means taking a systematic, individualized approach. You may be on the path to diagnosis and treatment, but there are a few steps still along the way. In the next chapters, I'll take you through them. My hope is that by the time you get a diagnosis for your child—*if you get a diagnosis*—you will have more than a label. You will have a clear understanding of your child's developmental strengths and weaknesses, a unique developmental profile. That profile will be the key to getting your child the help she needs.

What if you are no longer worried about your child, because she is meeting key milestones? Keep reading anyway, at least through the next chapter. It's about developmental screening, an essential part of every child's health care.

Chapter Four

Formal Screening

No one knows your child better than you do. If you are concerned about her development, there's probably a good reason. Likewise, if you feel virtually certain that she is on a healthy developmental path—especially now that you know more about key milestones—you probably are right, too. But before you get diagnosis and treatment for your child, if that is warranted, or a clean bill of health, if that is appropriate, you need more information. You need to have your child's development formally screened, by a professional.

In a perfect world, you wouldn't have to ask for developmental screening. It would be a routine part of every well-child visit, especially in the first three years. But, sadly, it is not. Only about 15 percent of pediatricians say they always use a formal developmental screening tool. Many who do screen use unproven methods or fail to screen at every visit. And many more say they rely simply on their "clinical judgment"—in other words, they think they know a child in trouble when they see one. Study after study shows the result of this haphazard approach: pediatricians and other primary care providers fail to identify 70 to 80 percent of young children with developmental delays and mental illnesses. These overlooked children and their families pay an enormous cost in lost potential.

And our entire society pays, financially and otherwise, for making these children wait.

Increasingly, medical advisory groups, including the American Academy of Pediatrics and the American Academy of Neurology, recognize this and recommend routine screening and surveillance. Medicaid requires it for the children it covers. And yet, most doctors still don't do it, often citing a lack of time, training, or reimbursement—or a continuing faith in their ability to recognize developmental warning signs without formal screening.

Remember, doctors know a lot, but very few of them specialize in recognizing atypical development. In fact, studies show they are surprisingly poor at spotting developmental problems through informal observation. Expecting your doctor to find a developmental delay without doing any screening is like expecting him to discover your child is anemic without even testing his blood. He might guess right—but you wouldn't want to bet your child's health on it.

Screening 101

So you may have to insist that your child be screened. Before you do, though, you should understand what screening is and is not. A developmental screening test, quite simply, is a set of questions or brief observations that a professional can use to separate children into two groups: those who are at risk for a developmental disorder, and those who are not. A screening test does not confirm that a child has a disorder, nor does it diagnose a specific disorder. But it does identify most children who are showing signs of delay and who should get further evaluation.

Over the years, researchers have come up with a number of screening tools, relying on different combinations of questions and observations. Each of the tests has particular strengths and weaknesses. The best are inexpensive, can be administered quickly and easily in a variety of settings, and work for children from any cultural or socioeconomic background. They also rely heavily on information from parents—the best source.

None of the screening tests are 100 percent accurate: it is possible for a child with healthy development to "fail" a screening test; it is also possible for a child who has delays to "pass" it. Most professionals consider a screening test a success if it can accurately classify 70 to 80 percent of children. But there's a catch: a test that is extremely good at finding children who do have developmental delays—one that is highly "sensitive," in the jargon of test experts—may also falsely raise concerns about some children who don't have delays. Likewise, a test that rarely misclassifies developmentally healthy children—a test the experts call highly "specific"—may miss many children who are at risk. Ideally, a test would be both sensitive (picking up almost all the children who need help) and specific (picking up only the children who need help). But sometimes there's a trade-off.

And, here, I have a strong preference: I believe that you should insist on having your child screened with a test that is highly sensitive—that is, a test that is highly likely to alert you to any developmental delay. To me, the most important thing is to maximize the chance that a child with a developmental delay or disorder will be recognized, evaluated, and put into an effective intervention program at the earliest possible moment. Along the way, a few children who have no delays or disorders will also be referred for further evaluation and found to be just fine. That is an acceptable trade-off. Luckily, though, there are some tests that are quite sensitive and quite specific. Those are the ones I recommend most often.

> The thing is, if you get referred, there's no down side. If the child doesn't need it, so what? If they do need it, the child could progress so much more. I've said it before: I believe, for a fact, that Chris would be further along than he is today if he'd had that early intervention. He lost out. . . . We've seen kids that were very involved. They got that early

verification. They got screened. They got referred at eighteen months, which is very rare, and those children, many of them are mainstreamed today.

Gary Weitzen of New Jersey, father of Chris,
diagnosed with autism at age three

I have another strong preference: I want all children to be screened with comprehensive tests designed to measure social, emotional, and communication skills, as well as motor, self-help, and cognitive skills, behavior, and temperament. To put it simply, a screening test that looks for delays in relating and communicating is the most likely to find them. As one parent says: "The questions the doctors ask don't cover what's actually wrong."

The pediatrician never had us fill out any questionnaire. And my daughter had enough normal behavior that she came in under the radar. For example, the doctor asked how many words she had, but he didn't ask how she was using the words. And I told him about how she liked to line up toys, but I just didn't think to clue him in to the intensity— that it was 24/7.

Becky Wilson of Oregon, mother of Zoë, diagnosed
at age four with developmental language disorder
and "regulatory disorder with autistic behaviors"

Recommended Screening Tools

I've made it my business over the past few years to study available developmental screening tools and learn which do the best job. A number of very good ones are now widely available. A complete list, which will be updated as new tools are tested and introduced, is at www.firstsigns.org.

One especially valuable tool is the Communication and Symbolic Behavior Scales Developmental Profile (CSBS DP) Infant-Toddler Checklist, devised by the First Signs advisers Amy M.

Wetherby and Barry M. Prizant. This is a simple twenty-four-item questionnaire that most parents can complete in five to ten minutes. It can be used for children between the ages of six months and twenty-four months. It provides multiple choices, a feature I like because it allows parents to express some degree of uncertainty. And, most important, it is specifically designed to detect warning signs in two groups of children:

- those with language and learning disorders, behavior disorders, mental retardation, and autism spectrum disorders
- those who have more specific problems with hearing, speech production, or the muscles in the face and mouth used for speech

Look through the checklist. You'll see that the questions are about the very skills—gestures, sounds, words, play—that a child needs to communicate and participate in the social world. The checklist is copyrighted, but Brookes Publishing allows free downloads (from www.brookespublishing.com).

CSBS DP CSBS DP Infant-Toddler Checklist

Child's name: _____   Date of birth: _____ Date filled out: _____

Was birth premature?_____   If yes, how many weeks premature? _____

Filled out by: _____   Relationship to child: _____

Instructions for caregivers: This checklist is designed to identify different aspects of development in infants and toddlers. Many behaviors that develop before children talk may indicate whether or not a child will have difficulty learning to talk. This checklist should be completed by a caregiver when the child is between **6 and 24 months** of age to determine whether a referral for an evaluation is needed. The caregiver may be either a parent or another person who nurtures the child daily. Please check all the choices that best describe your child's behavior. If you are not sure, please choose the closest response based on your experience. **Children at your child's age are not necessarily expected to use all the behaviors listed.**

Emotion and Eye Gaze

1. Do you know when your child is happy and when your child is upset?

❏ Not Yet ❏ Sometimes ❏ Often

2. When your child plays with toys, does he/she look at you to see if you are watching? ❑ Not Yet ❑ Sometimes ❑ Often

3. Does your child smile or laugh while looking at you? ❑ Not Yet ❑ Sometimes ❑ Often

4. When you look at and point to a toy across the room, does your child look at it? ❑ Not Yet ❑ Sometimes ❑ Often

Communication

5. Does your child let you know that he/she needs help or wants an object out of reach? ❑ Not Yet ❑ Sometimes ❑ Often

6. When you are not paying attention to your child, does he/she try to get your attention? ❑ Not Yet ❑ Sometimes ❑ Often

7. Does your child do things just to get you to laugh? ❑ Not Yet ❑ Sometimes ❑ Often

8. Does your child try to get you to notice interesting objects—just to get you to look at the objects, not to get you to do anything with them? ❑ Not Yet ❑ Sometimes ❑ Often

Gestures

9. Does your child pick up objects and give them to you? ❑ Not Yet ❑ Sometimes ❑ Often

10. Does your child show objects to you without giving you the object? ❑ Not Yet ❑ Sometimes ❑ Often

11. Does your child wave to greet people? ❑ Not Yet ❑ Sometimes ❑ Often

12. Does your child point to objects? ❑ Not Yet ❑ Sometimes ❑ Often

13. Does your child nod his/her head to indicate yes? ❑ Not Yet ❑ Sometimes ❑ Often

Sounds

14. Does your child use sounds or words to get attention or help? ❑ Not Yet ❑ Sometimes ❑ Often

15. Does your child string sounds together, such as "uh oh," "mama," "gaga," "bye-bye," "bada"? ❑ Not Yet ❑ Sometimes ❑ Often

16. About how many of the following consonant sounds does your child use: "ma," "na," "ba," "da," "ga," "wa," "la," "ya," "sa," "sha"? ❑ None ❑ 1-2 ❑ 3-4 ❑ 5-8 ❑ over 8

Words

17. About how many different words does your child use meaningfully that you recognize (such as "baba" for bottle; "gaggie" for doggie)? ❑ None ❑ 1-3 ❑ 4-10 ❑ 11-30 ❑ over 30

18. Does your child put two words together (for example, "more cookie," "bye-bye Daddy")? ❑ Not Yet ❑ Sometimes ❑ Often

Understanding

19. When you call your child's name, does he/she respond by looking or turning
toward you? ☐ Not Yet ☐ Sometimes ☐ Often

20. About how many different words or phrases does your child understand without
gestures? For example, if you say "Where's your tummy?," "Where's Daddy?,"
"Give me the ball," or "Come here," without showing or pointing, your child will
respond appropriately. ☐ None ☐ 1-3 ☐ 4-10 ☐ 11-30 ☐ over 3

Object Use

21. Does your child show interest in playing with a variety of objects?
☐ Not Yet ☐ Sometimes ☐ Often

22. About how many of the following objects does your child use appropriately: cup,
bottle, bowl, spoon, comb or brush, toothbrush, washcloth, ball, toy vehicle, toy
telephone? ☐ None ☐ 1-2 ☐ 3-4 ☐ 5-8 ☐ over 8

23. About how many blocks (or rings) does your child stack?
Stacks ☐ None ☐ 2 blocks ☐ 3-4 blocks ☐ 5 or more

24. Does your child pretend to play with toys (for example, feed a stuffed animal, put a
doll to sleep, put an animal figure in a vehicle)?
☐ Not Yet ☐ Sometimes ☐ Often

Do you have any concerns about your child's development?
☐ Yes ☐ No If yes, please describe on back.

Another screening tool I recommend is the Parents' Evaluation
of Developmental Status (PEDS) shown on the next page and
offered online by Forepath (see Resources). This is a ten-item quiz
that most parents can complete in two to ten minutes. The PEDS
can be used for children from birth through age eight and it cov
ers communication, motor, thinking, and self-help skills, along
with behavior. The PEDS, developed by Frances P. Glascoe, a First
Signs adviser who is a professor of pediatrics, differs from many
other screening tools because it does not look for specific milestones. Instead, it probes for parents' concerns in various areas of
development. The idea is to tap the power of parental observation
to identify children at risk.

If you decide to complete the CSBS DP Infant-Toddler Checklist, the PEDS, or both, the next step is crucial: take the completed forms to your child's doctor. Parents who take the PEDS test online will get a letter intended for their child's physician, along with the test results. If the doctor is unfamiliar with these screening tools, refer him to the First Signs website, where he will find information and links that allow him to interpret the results.

Other screening tools worth discussing with your child's doctor include the Ages and Stages Questionnaires (ASQ), for children between four and sixty months old, and the Greenspan Social-Emotional Growth Chart, which can be used for children from birth to age forty-two months.

Test ID 1112 fetched

Record of PEDS Responses

Child's Name: Jerri Smith Parent's name: Linda Smith

Child's DOB: 2003-07-20 Child's Age group: 18-23 Months Date of test: 2005-03-20

PEDS Score: Path A. High Risk M-CHAT result: fail

Please list any concerns about your child's learning, development, and behavior

She is extremely shy and hates loud noise. She started to talk early but then stopped all speech a few months later. Although she started up again it is not like it should be. She bounces off walls, laughing, but it is odd and very tuned out.

Do you have any concerns about how your child talks and makes speech sounds?

Response was "Yes"

Comment: She speaks slowly in a halting monotone as if she is searching for words. She almost never uses gestures and tends to use some words over and over out of context.

Do you have any concerns about how your child understands what you say?

Response was "Yes"

Comment: I sometimes think that she doesn't follow directions because she doesn't understand what is being asked of her. It is very hard for her to look at your face and read your expressions.

> **Do you have any concerns about how your child uses his or her hands and fingers to do things?**

Response was "A little"

Comment: She used to keep her hands in a fist and wouldn't open them but has gotten better and now seems fascinated with small objects and especially their moving parts.

> **Do you have any concerns about how your child uses his or her arms and legs?**

Response was "A little"

Comment: She tends to walk on tiptoes. I think this is because she doesn't really watch us walk or try to imitate the way other people move.

> **Do you have any concerns about how your child behaves?**

Response was "Yes"

Comment: Yes, she hardly seems to notice others and prefers to remain by herself.

> **Do you have any concerns about how your child is learning to do things for himself/herself?**

Response was "Yes"

Comment: She will not feed herself and doesn't attempt to dress herself.

> **Do you have any concerns about how your child is learning preschool or school skills?**

Response was "No"

Comment: I think she's too young for this but already seems very interested in letters and words and tends to look at these instead of pictures in books.

> **Please list any other comments**

Comment: I wondered if she could hear or sees OK but her pediatrician said she's fine. Sometimes she seems to be in pain especially when distressed.

Scored by Forepath
The online implementation of the PEDS child development screen

About "The Denver"

Some of you may decide not to try these screening tools because your doctor already has screened your child. Maybe she even screens at every visit. That sounds good, but here's a caution: chances are your doctor is using something called the Denver Developmental Screening Test–II or the related Revised Denver Prescreening Developmental Questionnaire. Doctors call this set of tests simply the Denver.

The Denver tests have been around for decades, are widely distributed—and have never been proven to accurately identify children at risk for developmental delays. Attempts by researchers to determine the Denver's accuracy have produced varied results. One study found it missing almost half of children who turned out to have developmental disorders. In any case, the Denver is poorly designed for well-visit use: in its complete form, it takes at least twenty minutes to administer and requires the physician to actually observe a number of skills in the child. For instance, a child might be required to stack some number of blocks, draw a picture, and show that he knows the meaning of several key words. Now, consider the fact that the average well-child visit lasts fourteen to eighteen minutes and that the average child wishes it were even shorter—and you see the problem. The test takes too long and it requires children to perform in a high-stress situation. In practice, few doctors use the full Denver. Instead, they pick just a few items to test on each age group—and then, they guess at what the results mean. That makes the test invalid. Your child deserves better than that.

Other Key Screening Tests

When screening tools like the CSBS DP Infant-Toddler Checklist and the PEDS suggest that a child has a developmental delay, that child should get a full developmental evaluation. Likewise, if your child has passed some screening tests but you are still worried, additional testing is quite justified. But before comprehensive testing can reveal a child's full developmental profile, it often makes sense to run a few additional screening tests—tests that may offer further clues to the nature of a child's difficulties. In particular, every child showing delays in language, communication, or social skills should be screened for

- hearing problems
- lead poisoning
- autism spectrum disorders

Why Your Child Needs a Hearing Test

The relationship between a child's hearing, his communication skills, and his overall development is complex. A child who appears to have a language delay or poor social skills may, in fact, have a hearing problem that is the root of his other problems. Likewise, a child who sometimes seems deaf—because he responds so little to the world around him—may turn out to have a perfect ability to hear sounds, but a severe problem with understanding and acting on the things he hears. And then there's the perplexing situation in which a child seems to ignore some sounds, like his parents' voices, but to react strongly (either in a negative or positive way) to others, such as the vacuum cleaner, sirens, or music. The first step in sorting out these issues is an audiological screening exam—a hearing test.

What's Involved: Your child's doctor can refer you to a nearby audiology clinic, probably in a local hospital, for this kind of testing. Or, if you are getting a full developmental evaluation from an early intervention program or school system, they may refer you to a clinic.

Wherever the testing is done, expect a child-friendly experience. Often, your child can simply sit on your lap while a skilled technician assesses her hearing using toys, puppets, lights, and recorded sounds. But call ahead and find out the details so that you can prepare your child. For instance, she probably will need to wear headphones, so you might want to let her try some at home, maybe with some favorite music. Also, some children—especially children who have had medical problems—are unhappy about visiting a hospital or anything that looks like a medical office. So, let your child know where you are going and what you will do there. If it's a hospital, emphasize that you will come home afterward.

Why Your Child Needs Lead Screening

Almost any developmental delay—including delays in language and thinking abilities—could be a symptom of lead poisoning. The

American Academy of Pediatrics says one million U.S. children have elevated levels of lead in their blood. This is a condition that can cause anemia, hearing loss, kidney failure, seizures, and even death; both physical and mental development can be severely affected. So a simple blood test for lead is essential in any child with a developmental delay. If a child turns out to have high lead levels, parents can then find the source of the lead (often it's lead-based paint in an older home, or contaminated soil around abandoned industrial areas) and either eliminate it or move their family away from it. The child can also get medical treatment to reduce the damage.

What's Involved: Your child will need to go to a doctor's office or clinic for a blood test. Usually, blood will be taken from a vein in the child's arm, though some doctors do a finger-prick test as a preliminary step (if that's positive, they get the larger sample to confirm the results). Blood tests can be tough for small children. After all, no child likes needles, and some are terrified of them. And a blood test takes longer than a shot: a child has to sit still while a nurse or lab worker finds a vein, inserts a needle, and fills a tube with blood. Some children strongly object to this kind of handling and may have difficulty communicating their distress in any way but an all-out meltdown.

The best advice I can give you is to consider your child and prepare him as much as you can. For some children that means a lot of talking, play-acting with dolls, and maybe an advance visit to the clinic to talk about what will happen. Others, like my own daughter, have such a heightened anxiety about needles that it's best not to talk about them ahead of time. One thing to keep in mind: the lab technician may ask you to hold your child still, which is sometimes a two-parent job. If only one parent can go and you have the choice, make it the physically stronger one. And be sure to reward your child for any sign of cooperation during the test. Afterward, give him a little prize: it may help get him through the door the next time he needs blood work or a medical procedure.

Why Your Child Needs Autism Screening

Ideally, doctors would routinely screen all children for development in all areas and for specific signs of autism and other developmental disorders. That's not happening yet, despite support for the idea from leading medical groups. But, when other more general developmental screening tests raise concerns, an autism screening test is essential. Like other screening tests, these cannot provide a diagnosis. But these quick, easy-to-administer tests can help you and your doctor learn whether your child is showing delays or deficits in the three core areas related to autism: social skills, communication, and behaviors and interests. Combined with the results of other, more general screening tests, an autism screening test can help you choose the next, best steps for your child.

What's Involved: Valid, reliable tests are available for children sixteen months and older (and screening tests for younger children are under development). The doctor may ask you a few questions and then spend a few minutes observing and interacting with your child, looking to see how he communicates, how socially engaged he is, and whether he exhibits certain repetitive behaviors or limited, obsessive interests. Or the test may consist entirely of a parent questionnaire. If you know a doctor will be screening your child for autism with observations and interactions, make sure the testing takes place on a day when your child is well rested and not sick. And pay attention to how the doctor conducts the observation: it should take at least five minutes and include skilled attempts to engage the child in back-and-forth communication and play.

The autism screening tool I recommend most often is the Modified Checklist for Autism in Toddlers (M-CHAT). This is a fairly new test, but early studies suggest it is both highly sensitive and specific: it correctly identifies children with and without autism spectrum disorders more than 90 percent of the time. The test consists of twenty-three questions for parents and is included here. However, after completing the checklist and scoring, share the results with your child's doctor. The M-CHAT is intended for children who are between the ages of sixteen and forty-eight months and may prove valid for children even younger; studies are continuing to find the best age at which to use the test.

A comprehensive screening questionnaire is very helpful, because it asks so many more questions than a doctor can do in a fifteen-minute well visit. Even more important, it gives a parent some direction as to what signs to look for. James's autism diagnosis and treatment were delayed by six months, simply because his doctor only pointed out one sign of his developmental delays to us, which was not enough for us to take seriously. We thought our little angel was just a bit less than perfect.

Joy Johnson of Maryland, mother of
two boys with autism

M-CHAT

Please fill out the following about how your child usually is. Please try to answer every question. If the behavior is rare (e.g., you've seen it once or twice), please answer as if the child does not do it.

1. Does your child enjoy being swung, bounced on your knee, etc.?	Yes	No
2. Does your child take an interest in other children?	Yes	No
3. Does your child like climbing on things, such as up stairs?	Yes	No
4. Does your child enjoy playing peek-a-boo/hide-and-seek?	Yes	No
5. Does your child ever pretend, for example, to talk on the phone or take care of dolls, or pretend other things?	Yes	No
6. Does your child ever use his/her index finger to point, to ask for something?	Yes	No
7. Does your child ever use his/her index finger to point, to indicate interest in something?	Yes	No
8. Can your child play properly with small toys (e.g., cars or bricks) without just mouthing, fiddling, or dropping them?	Yes	No
9. Does your child ever bring objects over to you (parent) to show you something?	Yes	No
10. Does your child look you in the eye for more than a second or two?	Yes	No

---

11. Does your child ever seem oversensitive to noise? (e.g., plugging ears)   Yes   No

12. Does your child smile in response to your face or your smile?   Yes   No

13. Does your child imitate you? (e.g., you make a face—will your child imitate it?)   Yes   No

14. Does your child respond to his/her name when you call?   Yes   No

15. If you point at a toy across the room, does your child look at it?   Yes   No

16. Does your child walk?   Yes   No

17. Does your child look at things you are looking at?   Yes   No

18. Does your child make unusual finger movements near his/her face?   Yes   No

19. Does your child try to attract your attention to his/her own activity?   Yes   No

20. Have you ever wondered if your child is deaf?   Yes   No

21. Does your child understand what people say?   Yes   No

22. Does your child sometimes stare at nothing or wander with no purpose?   Yes   No

23. Does your child look at your face to check your reaction when faced with something unfamiliar?   Yes   No

© 1999 Diana Robins, Deborah Fein, and Marianne Barton
Please refer to: Robins, D., Fein, D., Barton, M., and Green, J. "The Modified Checklist for Autism in Toddlers: An Initial Study Investigating the Early Detection of Autism and Pervasive Developmental Disorders." *Journal of Autism and Developmental Disorders* 31 (2) (2001), 131–44.

M-CHAT Scoring Instructions

A child fails the checklist when two or more critical items are failed or when any three items are failed. Yes/no answers convert to pass/fail responses. Below are listed the failed responses for each item on the M-CHAT. Bold capitalized items are CRITICAL items.

Not all children who fail the checklist will meet criteria for a diagnosis on the autism spectrum. However, children who fail the checklist should be evaluated in more depth by the physician or referred for a developmental evaluation with a specialist.

1. No	6. No	11. Yes	16. No	21. No
2. **NO**	7. **NO**	12. No	17. No	22. Yes
3. No	8. No	13. **NO**	18. Yes	23. No
4. No	9. **NO**	14. **NO**	19. No	
5. No	10. No	15. **NO**	20. Yes	

A Word About Older Children

Children who have what some people call high-functioning autism—a relatively mild form of the disorder—often are not correctly diagnosed as toddlers or preschoolers because the signs are subtle or can be confused with other developmental disorders. This is also true for children with Asperger syndrome, an autism spectrum disorder in which children develop speech at a typical age and pace but have problems with back-and-forth communication and social skills, coupled with a limited set of interests and a tendency toward rigid behavior. There are several good screening tools designed for children over age four that can help to correctly identify these children. They are listed at www.firstsigns.org.

It's important to know, though, that children with these milder forms of autism can be recognized before age four, if parents and professionals know what to look for: the deficits in social skills, communication, behavior, and interests that characterize all autism spectrum disorders.

Screening for Other Disorders

In the course of screening your child for developmental delays, you may uncover clues that your child has any number of disorders. In fact, he may have more than one, or he may have an entirely different disorder than the one you were most worried about at the outset. Additional screening tests might help you sort out those clues and get your child quickly headed toward the right diagnoses and treatments. Depending on the child, these additional screening tests might look for signs of

- *attention deficit hyperactivity disorder.* A recommended screening test for this common condition is the ADHD Symptom Checklist.
- *childhood bipolar disorder.* This increasingly recognized mood disorder can be diagnosed in children as young as

three or four. A good screening tool for the disorder is Young Mania Rating Scale (YMRS).

• *temperament and behavior disorders.* A screening test called the Ages and Stages Questionnaire: Social, Emotional (ASQ:SE) uses parent responses to assess social and emotional development in children between six months and five years old

---

To Do Now

Take your first step toward becoming an advocate for children other than your own.

If you learn that your pediatrician does not routinely screen for developmental delays, urge that doctor to screen your child—and all children in his or her practice. With the tips and resources available at www.firstsigns.org, pediatricians can learn how to fit routine screening into their busy practices.

Spread the screening message further. Tell other parents, day care workers, and preschool teachers what you've learned about the value of routine screening. And, while you're at it, write a few letters, urging your insurance company, state lawmakers, and members of Congress to support changes that will make routine screening a reality for every child.

Chapter Five

Entering the Maze—
Getting Answers, Getting Help

At first, you hoped that you really were just an overanxious parent, or that your child's delays or differences would simply disappear. But now your own observations and formal screening by professionals have made it clear: your child does seem to have a developmental problem. And it's not going away. That can be a terrifying thought. Even worse is the fact that you don't yet know exactly what the problem is or how to help.

This is often the scariest time for parents. You look at your child and start to wonder: Will he ever have a "normal" life? If you suspect that your child has an autism spectrum disorder, mental retardation, a psychiatric disorder—any serious problem—you may be especially frightened. One of my most difficult moments came when early testing suggested that my daughter had delayed cognitive skills and the language and social skills of a baby less than half her age. She was only two years old, and I saw my dreams for her future slipping away. You, too, may spend sleepless nights imagining the very grimmest outcomes. And you may spend many of those wide-awake hours surfing the Internet, reading a confusing array of science, pseudoscience, and unfiltered parental chatter, wondering what, if anything, it all means for your child.

At first you have no idea what to do and you're hesitant to talk about it. You don't want people to know the degree of struggle that you're having. So you fall into a helpless and hopeless situation. You start fast-forwarding in your mind. . . . We were thinking, "My God, this kid is only three. What's going to happen to him in the next few years? Is he going to have to be institutionalized?"

Fred Wayne of Delaware, father of Derrick,
diagnosed with childhood bipolar disorder,
anxiety, and ADHD at age three

Often, parents get paralyzed at this point. They know something is wrong, but they don't want to face the finality of a diagnosis—and a label that might stick to their child forever. Or they know they should do something, but they don't know what. And it is always easier to wait—another day, another week, or another month.

But think again of your child, and of his growing, developing mind. He needs help now. And you are the only one who can get it for him. So take a deep breath and get out a phone and a pen. It's time to call in the cavalry.

Entering the Maze

Unfortunately, it's not as easy as calling 1-800-HELPMYKID. Instead, you may well find yourself making dozens of phone calls—to medical specialists, therapists, insurers, and public agencies. Along the way, you may find some helpful souls: perhaps an insurance clerk will go out of her way to answer your questions; maybe a nurse will make an extra call to get you into an overbooked specialist's office; perhaps you will find a doctor who will not only diagnose your child but also stop to ask how you are coping. But it's also quite likely that you will encounter your share of clueless clerks, mountainous waiting lists, pointless policies, and insensitive professionals. You also may bump into infuriating dead ends.

Meanwhile, you will spend hours wading through forms and bills, driving to and from appointments, and sitting in waiting rooms for what may seem like eternity.

Of course, you must navigate this complex process while juggling the rest of your life. Suddenly, a paying job may start to seem like something you have to fit in between your child's appointments. Keeping up any sort of social life may seem like a laughable luxury. And you may find yourself so busy trying to help your child that you suddenly realize you are hardly spending any time with her—not to mention any brothers or sisters she may have.

No doubt, the process of finding the right help will be time-consuming, complicated, and frustrating at times. Think of it as a maze: you are traveling toward a goal—the correct diagnosis and treatment for your child—but the path is unclear and full of false turns; getting to the goal quickly requires persistence, skill, knowledge, and, sometimes, a bit of luck. One key piece of advice: do not enter this maze alone.

Finding Partners: Personal and Professional

If you are part of a couple, when is the last time you and your partner went to one of your child's medical appointments together? I wouldn't be surprised if it was your baby's two-week checkup, or maybe even a prenatal ultrasound. And if you are a single parent, when is the last time another family member or friend accompanied you to one of your child's health care appointments? Maybe never? Now is the time to stop going by yourself. Once you know your child has a developmental delay, you need all the support you can get. Especially in the beginning, when you will be in unfamiliar and often frightening territory, you need an extra pair of hands, eyes, and ears at every appointment. And you need an extra set of shoulders to carry what can be a very heavy burden. Ideally, in a two-parent family, both parents will go to the appointments and meetings that could determine your child's future. When that's not possible—and, of course, sometimes it is not, particularly for parents whose jobs allow little flexibility—try to enlist another family member or close friend to be your partner in this process.

Grandparents can be ideal for this role. In my own case, my husband was not available for my daughter's appointments. But my mother—a retired school psychologist who was worried about Sarah even before I was—was eager to accompany us. I appreciated her support at the time and learned later on that it went even further than I knew. It turns out that when Sarah was about eighteen months old, a time when I was still denying the problem, my mother actually slipped out of the waiting room after Sarah's routine checkup, cornered our pediatrician, and told her that she was worried Sarah had autism. The pediatrician brushed her off. But my mother stayed involved, without terrifying me by blurting out her worst fears, and played a key role in getting Sarah properly diagnosed several months later.

That experience with the pediatrician illustrates another important point: primary care providers, the physicians and nurse practitioners who see children for routine care, can be great allies when your child is in developmental peril. Or they can be no help at all. Worse yet, they can be roadblocks. Now is the time to determine, once and for all, what kind of provider you have. You need an experienced professional ally. And you need to say goodbye to anyone who is an obstacle to your child's optimum care. Certainly that includes anyone who continues to deny your child's developmental delays. But also watch out for these two signs that you are dealing with a roadblocker:

- She confirms your worries with a screening test or acknowledges that your child is showing developmental Red Flags—but still tells you to "wait and see" how your child does over another few months.
- He says he shares your concerns and offers you some tips for helping your child—maybe a few strategies for prompting more speech—but declines to refer you to anyone else for further evaluation or treatment.

Incredibly, neither of these scenarios is rare. In fact, studies suggest that the majority of children who fail developmental screening tests are not immediately referred for further evaluation or treatment. That is simply unacceptable. If your child has failed a screening test or is showing Red Flags of developmental delay, tell your pediatrician you will not leave his office without at least two phone numbers: one for a specialist with expertise in diagnosing developmental and behavioral disorders and another for either your state's early intervention program or your local school district, depending on your child's age.

The Specialists: Who They Are

Ideally, your pediatrician will have a good idea of whom your child should see first. His opinion should be based on your child's specific characteristics and delays. Typically, the choices might include any of the following specialists:

Developmental and Behavioral Pediatricians. These are medical doctors (MDs) who specialize in treating the health problems of children with developmental and behavioral disorders. They are familiar with neurological problems, medications for brain disorders, and the latest research on early identification and treatment. They are accustomed to working closely with other specialists. However, there are relatively few of these doctors in any state, and they are in high demand. But it's worth asking your pediatrician to help you find one. They can find names through a search engine on the American Academy of Pediatrics website at www.aap.org.

Pediatric Neurologists. These are MDs who specialize in brain disorders. While some have a special interest in autism and other disorders of communicating and relating, many do not. The typical pediatric neurologist has a practice heavily focused on children with seizure disorders, cerebral palsy, and complex genetic conditions; they also see a lot of children with attention deficit hyperactivity disorder (ADHD). However, it's often wise for a child with other sorts of delays and disorders to see a neurologist, if only to rule out seizures and other treatable conditions that might be contributing factors.

Child Psychiatrists. These are MDs who have special expertise in clinical depression, anxiety disorders, ADHD, and other brain disorders that can affect how children think and behave. Some also have a special interest in autism and related disorders. Like other MDs, they can prescribe medication; they also can provide various forms of talk and play therapy. Some specialize in particular therapy techniques.

Child Psychologists. Child psychologists are not medical doctors and can't prescribe medication. But they can diagnose developmental and behavioral disorders, provide certain forms of therapy, and offer advice on coping, education strategies, and behavior management. Some specialize in particular therapy techniques and can help a family put together a comprehensive intervention plan and a team of providers.

Which of these specialists should be your child's first stop? Ideally, your primary care provider will have at least one individual in mind—someone in your community who specializes in the very delays or disorders suspected in your child. But, in practice, pediatricians often take a one-size-fits-all approach to referrals, sending every child with any sort of developmental delay to, say, the nearest neurologist—even if that neurologist is not a specialist in development. I've never forgotten my frustration at waiting weeks for Sarah to see a particular neurologist, only to find out that his primary interest was in a relatively rare seizure disorder that causes language loss. When he learned Sarah did not have that disorder—after a harrowing EEG (brainwave test) for which we were totally unprepared—he had absolutely nothing to offer us. No diagnosis. No further referrals. Despite his distinguished degrees and affiliations, he had no clue about how to diagnose an autism spectrum disorder. It would take me additional months to find a specialist who did.

In general, it's less important that your child see a doctor with a particular degree than that he see a doctor or other professional who devotes much of his practice to diagnosing and treating developmental and behavioral disorders. In one community, that best person might be a neurologist; in another, it might be a clinical psychologist. You will be far ahead of the game if your pediatrician knows the community well enough to know who that best person is. You'll be even further ahead if your pediatrician can give you more than one name. Then you can ask her:

- what she knows about the expertise of each of the professionals on the list
- who she recommends most highly for children with the disorders or delays suspected in your child
- who is likely to have the longest waiting list and whether she has any clout to help you to bypass the long wait

Then you can do some quick research yourself. Many hospitals and large medical practices have websites with detailed physician biographies. Go ahead and Google the specialists—keeping in mind that you don't need to be famous to be an excellent hands-on clinician.

If you are not satisfied that you are headed in the right direction, ask your pediatrician for other ideas. And—this is important—let the pediatrician know that you would be happy to see a specialist far from home, if that would get your child more expert care. It's just a fact of life that the best medical care in America is concentrated in urban areas and at major university medical centers. So if you live in a smaller city or a rural area, you may need to travel a little to get the expertise your child deserves. Even if you live near a big city, as I do, you will sometimes find that the top specialist you need for a particular problem is located hours away. I still drive Sarah four hours each way, once a month, to see one crucial member of her care team.

How to Get In Quickly

Once you know which specialist or specialists you should see first, start making calls. And expect to run into a waiting list or two. For some specialists, the wait might be six months, a year, or even more. As you know by now, that's far too long for you and your child to wait for help. So what do you do? Here's what I advise:

- Do not hang up without making an appointment. If this is a professional you really want to see, you probably still will want to see her six months or a year from now—even if you get an initial evaluation and/or treatment from someone else.
- Ask the receptionist what you can do to get in sooner. Often, overbooked practices keep a list of people who are willing to come in on short notice if someone else cancels an appointment, as happens constantly. One parent I know wanted to see an autism specialist who had a year-long waiting list. She told the doctor's staff that she and her child could be there on two hours' notice. Sure enough, they got in within two weeks.
- Call back regularly to check for openings, without making a nuisance of yourself. Be persistent but not frantic. (One especially persistent parent I know saw a nationally renowned specialist at a conference. She was determined that her child would see this doctor, who was taking no new patients. So she trailed this semiretired gentleman from the podium to the door of the men's restroom. She might have accompanied him to the stall if he hadn't said, "Here, hold my briefcase outside and we'll talk when I'm done." They did talk, and her son soon got an appointment.)
- Don't hesitate to stress the age of your child and the sense of urgency you feel. With the increased emphasis on early

n, many clinics now are going out of their way
very youngest children first.

ar pediatrician or family physician if they can place
onal call to the specialist. One friend who suspected
le seizures as well as developmental delays in her baby
was put on a one-month waiting list by a neurologist's
office. Her pediatrician called and got the baby in the next
day. It turned out that he was having brain-damaging
seizures that needed immediate treatment.

- If you can't get in to see your top specialist right away, ask
her staff to recommend someone you might see while you
are waiting. Describe the kinds of problems your child
has—delayed speech or underdeveloped social skills, for
example—and ask who might be able to help right away.

Along the way, remember this: though you ultimately do want a
diagnosis for your child, the diagnosis is not as important as the intervention. And you can start the intervention without an exact diagnosis.

Building the Team

In addition to the specialists already listed, you might start your
child's team with a variety of other professionals, including:

Speech/Language Pathologists (SLPs) help people learn to
speak or improve their ability to speak. Many practices specialize in
children. Often, you can get a child with obvious speech delays or
impairments started on speech therapy well before you get through
the process of having him formally diagnosed.

Occupational Therapists (OTs) can help people improve fine
motor and self-help skills, such as writing, drawing, dressing, handling utensils, and using toys. These therapists also can work on
the mouth muscles involved in speech and eating. Some provide
listening therapies for children with auditory processing disorders.
And some further specialize in sensory integration, the ability to

process and learn from sensations, such as movement, touch, sights, sounds, odors, and tastes. Difficulties with sensation are quite common among children with autism and related disorders.

Physical Therapists (PTs) can help a child who is behind in large motor skills, such as balancing, walking, running, climbing, and using playground equipment. Children who have weak muscles or overall coordination problems can benefit from physical therapy.

Behavior Therapists are experts in behavior modification and can come from a variety of disciplines, including psychology and special education. Some help parents design and implement plans to improve specific behaviors, such as tantrums or biting. Others design broader skill-building programs for children with autism and other developmental disorders and help parents assemble teams of providers trained in complementary techniques.

DIR (Developmental, Individual Difference, Relationship-based approach)/Floortime clinicians also come from a variety of disciplines, including psychology, and specialize in teaching parents how to interact with their child in a way that will build the child's social, communication, and thinking skills. They can also help parents assemble a team that includes other professionals trained in complementary techniques.

Play Therapists help children with emotional or communication problems through individual or group play sessions. Some psychologists, social workers, and other professionals are certified in this specialty.

Social Workers offer resource information, counseling, and practical support to families coping with crisis. These mental health workers are found in private practice and in public agencies.

Not all children with developmental delays and disorders need to see every brand of specialist or get every type of therapy. And the specialist who will turn out to be most important to your child's success may not appear on this list. For example, many children with disorders of communicating and relating have other overlapping or coexisting health problems, including allergies and gastrointestinal disorders. Many parents find that treating those problems is crucial to their child's well-being and optimal development. So seeing an allergist, a gastroenterologist, or a nutritionist may be just as important for your child as seeing a speech therapist. It all depends on your child's unique needs.

But it's almost impossible for any parent to sort out the priorities alone. You need a professional partner—usually a pediatrician, family physician, or developmental pediatrician—who knows your child's full history and continues to follow him as you start the intervention process. Whether you need a referral, help sorting out conflicting advice, or a sounding board in a crisis, that professional should be there for you and your child.

Once you know what kind of services you need, you also should seek recommendations for particular specialists from other parents, preschool teachers, and other knowledgeable people. In general, it's best not to just pluck names out of the phone book.

As you begin to gather a team, it's your job to keep the members working together toward the same goal: the best possible outcome for your child. That means that each member of the team needs to know who the others are, what they are doing, and, most important, what they have learned about your child. So when the occupational therapist gives you a written evaluation of your child's motor skills, make sure that any other therapists, doctors, and teachers see the report, too. And when a nutritionist suggests dietary supplements, let your primary care provider and other team members know what you are trying. They may not always agree that it is a good idea—but they should always know about it.

You may find that some members of your team can be very territorial when they sense others on "their" turf. Listen respectfully if and when you run into disagreements about your child's treatment. And consider carefully the varying expertise of those involved. But also consider how respectfully the professionals are listening to you, and to each other. You only want to work with people who can work together in the best interest of your child. If that's not happening, make a change.

You do need to listen to the professionals. But if you think something is wrong, you need to speak up and not be so nice all of the time.

Danielle Draut of California, mother of triplet boys—two diagnosed with autism-related disorders and one with impaired hearing

Of course, one of your biggest challenges will be keeping everything straight yourself. So this is the time to get organized:

- Keep a master calendar—paper or electronic, whichever works for you—and make sure every appointment goes into it the moment you schedule it.
- Start a phone log, showing the names and numbers of everyone you call, along with a brief note on the subject you discussed.
- Start a three-ring binder or accordion folder with sections to file your reports, notes, lab results, bills, and insurance forms. Some people like to carry it from appointment to appointment so they have easy access to any information they need.
- Keep an updated list of the names, addresses, phone numbers, and e-mail addresses for each of your child's team members and an updated list of your child's medications, vitamins, and nutritional supplements. Having all this key information in one place will be extremely useful when you find yourself filling out the inevitable mountain of forms that accompanies evaluation and treatment. Share this information with every new team member.

Another word about all those forms: almost every professional you see will want to gather a complete developmental history of your child. They'll want to know what her birth was like, when she achieved key milestones, and when you first saw any behaviors that troubled you. And many will want you to fill out an extensive questionnaire on this topic. Look at these forms not as a chore but as an opportunity. This is a chance to help the professionals pinpoint your child's strengths and weaknesses and to begin to see the patterns that form your child's unique developmental profile. That profile will point you toward a particular diagnosis and set of interventions.

Pull out any baby memory books, photographs, or videos that might help you to reconstruct your child's earliest months. Whenever you make an appointment, ask for any forms to be sent to you in advance. You don't want to be sitting in a waiting room and entertaining your child while trying to compose an impromptu essay about her development. Also, with the forms in hand, you can ask another family member or friend—a spouse, grandparent, or nanny, for example—to offer his or her input.

In Sarah's case, my mother went above and beyond helping me fill out the forms. When we were about to get Sarah's first full developmental evaluation, she offered to write a letter, outlining her observations of Sarah's development. That letter did not contain the term "autism spectrum disorder" or "PDD." But here's an excerpt:

> To date, I have never heard her call Mommy or
> Daddy. . . . She does not substitute gestures for language in
> an attempt to communicate with others. In fact, she seems
> not to feel the need to communicate, but instead seems to
> prefer solitary play. She is usually content to stay in her
> playpen and play with a few toys. In general, her play is
> often very repetitive and at times ritualistic.

My mother also mentioned that Sarah rarely smiled at us, made eye contact, or responded to her name. Mom was very wise: she didn't want to be the first person to label her granddaughter as having a form of autism, but she also was determined that the professionals with the power to help would not miss the unmistakable signs. And they didn't. That letter helped my daughter get help quickly for her most pressing problems, months before she was formally diagnosed. I am still grateful for it.

Early Intervention Programs

Up to now, I've been talking about professionals in private practice whom you may consult when seeking diagnosis and treatment for your child. But it's every bit as important that you take full advantage of the publicly funded programs that are available in every state to help young children at risk for developmental delays and disorders. Under federal law, states must provide these services.

For children under age three (and in some states through age five), these services fall under the banner of "Early Intervention." The agencies that provide Early Intervention services vary from state to state: in your state, the responsible agency may be the department of public health, the department of education, or the department of human services. But any good pediatrician's office should know exactly whom to call in your community. You can also get contact numbers from the National Early Childhood Technical Assistance Center (www.nectac.org/contact/ptccoord.asp).

Once you know whom to call, make the call right away. You don't have to wait until your child has a diagnosis and you don't need a referral from a physician. If you are concerned that your child may have developmental delays, you are entitled to a free evaluation from your state's Early Intervention program. Just make the call and get the process started.

The details vary from state to state, but the usual practice is to assign the family a service coordinator, who will then collect additional information and work with you to determine whether a multidisciplinary evaluation is needed. This evaluation will focus on specific developmental areas, including cognitive, language, motor, social, emotional, behavioral, and self-help skills. Often a team of professionals—including an educator, a social worker, a speech/language therapist, and an occupational or physical therapist—will come to your home to test and observe your child. The team will then put together a report that will determine whether your child is eligible for Early Intervention services.

Each state has its own standards for eligibility, but all states must provide services to infants and toddlers who have developmental delays or who have a diagnosed mental or physical condition likely to result in such delays (for example, Down syndrome or premature birth). Delays are classified as follows.

- Adaptive delays concern self-help skills such as dressing and feeding.
- Cognitive delays involve thinking skills, including the ability to absorb, process, and understand information.
- Communicative delays impair the ability to understand and use language, follow directions, and make needs known.
- Physical delays involve gross and fine motor skills, vision, hearing, sensory integration, and motor planning (the ability to plan, organize, and carry out actions).
- Social and emotional delays impede the ability to interact with children, adults, and the environment.

Some states also provide services to children who aren't yet showing delays, but are at risk because of various biological or environmental factors, including poverty.

Once your child is declared eligible, you will sit down with the service coordinator and other members of the Early Intervention team to write an "Individualized Family Service Plan" (IFSP). This report should detail your child's developmental strengths and weaknesses, your family's goals for your child, and a plan for working toward those goals.

What services are offered at this point can vary widely from state to state and from child to child. The entire plan might consist of a monthly visit by an early-education specialist who will teach you how to stimulate your child; it might consist of a weekly playgroup;

or it might call for a much more extensive program of therapy and parent training. Ideally, these differences would reflect children's differing needs. In practice, though, they often reflect the professional attitudes, knowledge, and resources of the particular agency involved. So be prepared to argue that your child needs more than is being offered. In many cases, this will require getting a diagnosis from a private clinician. Some states automatically offer more extensive services to children with certain diagnoses, including autism spectrum disorders. If you still are unable to get adequate services, you can file an appeal with your state's lead Early Intervention agency.

> They had a wonderful program where they offered us up to forty hours of services if we wanted it. It was amazing how available they were to us and how much they offered us.
>
> *Susan Sutherland of Massachusetts, mother of Evan, diagnosed with PDD-NOS just before age three*

> They gave our older son just two hours a week at their center. Eventually they increased it to three. At the time, we thought it was pretty good because we just didn't know any better.
>
> *Joy Johnson of Maryland, mother of two boys with autism*

In some states, the services you receive from Early Intervention will cost your family nothing. Many states require you to pay part of the cost, with your share based on your income. Private insurers and Medicaid may pick up part of the cost, as well.

One important thing to know: While the people who work for Early Intervention programs can evaluate your child and provide services, they are not in the business of diagnosing children. They are not medical professionals. In fact, many are told to avoid labeling, both because babies and toddlers may overcome their delays and because many parents may be upset by certain labels.

rly Intervention wouldn't tell us anything. They would
er say the words. Finally when my son was three, I took
m to a private speech therapist. After one session, the private therapist told me it was pretty clear he had apraxia. I
went to his Early Intervention therapist and she said that
was what she had always thought! If I'd known earlier, I
could have done things differently and gotten the real
intense therapy that made a difference much earlier.

Kathy Bauer of Pennsylvania, mother of two
children diagnosed with speech apraxia (speech
delays caused by motor planning problems)

I naively assumed that if there was anything seriously
wrong with Brian, someone at Early Intervention would say
something. . . . I guessed later that everybody but us,
including the receptionist, knew he had autism.

Ann Guay of Massachusetts, whose son was
diagnosed with autism at age three

In some Early Intervention agencies, people may be more willing to steer you toward a diagnosis, in the belief, which I share, that
a diagnosis will increase the likelihood of your child getting the
most appropriate help.

Sarah's Early Intervention coordinator was the first person to
suggest she might have "PDD"—after I asked her, point blank, what
she thought the problem might be. I don't remember whether I
then asked her what PDD was, or whether she gave me an answer
I could comprehend. But I do remember calling my mother and
asking her to explain. She had been waiting for that call. That
night, on the phone, Mom explained to me that PDD was "pervasive developmental disorder," a term often used for autism spectrum disorders. The coordinator's opinion was not an official
diagnosis, of course. But I was devastated. I also was on my way to
finding the right help for my daughter.

School System Services

Most state Early Intervention programs provide services only to children younger than three (a few serve children up to age five). But, under federal law, school systems take over when Early Intervention ends. Their responsibility is to offer every disabled child a "free appropriate public education" through an "individualized education program (IEP)."

The key words here are "appropriate" and "individualized." What's appropriate for one child—say, a preschool class for children of varying abilities that meets a few mornings a week—may not be appropriate for all. Many children with disorders of communicating and relating need a much more intense program than the one-size-fits-all classes offered in many communities. But, as with Early Intervention programs, getting what's right for your child may require some negotiation. In some cases, it requires legal action. Go into the process hoping for a quick, painless agreement, but prepared to fight, if necessary, for the help your child needs. Keep in mind that if the school system has no existing program that meets your child's needs, it will need to create one, send your child for services in another district, or pay for private services.

And here's an important tip: never say that you are seeking the "best" or the "optimum" program for your child. The law requires only that it be "appropriate." As one friend of mine says, "You can ask for a Cadillac, but they only owe you a Ford." The key is to prove that what school administrators see as a fancy Cadillac—say, forty hours a week of intense one-on-one teaching and therapy—is actually the basic program your child needs to make adequate progress.

Here are some more tips for starting the process on the right foot.

- If your child is already three years old or more, contact the special education coordinator at your local school system right away. If you don't know whom to call, ask your neighborhood elementary school. You don't need a doctor's referral or any diagnosis to ask the school system to evaluate your child.

- If your child is younger than three, start with Early Intervention, but contact your local school system at least six months before your child will become eligible for school services (at thirty months for systems that take children at age three). As your child approaches age three, the Early Intervention service coordinator will help you with the transition from Early Intervention to a preschool program and/or other services needed by your child and family.

- Talk to other parents in your community who get services through the school system. You often can meet other parents through Early Intervention support groups and through other traditional and online groups. And don't hesitate to strike up conversations with the other parents you see in the waiting rooms of local speech therapists and OTs. You'll find at least a few who are eager to exchange stories about the school system.

- If possible, get an independent evaluation of your child before agreeing on an IEP with the school system. Otherwise, your child's program will be based entirely on the findings of school personnel, who vary tremendously in their ability to thoroughly and accurately assess children with developmental delays. And keep in that mind that, despite the requirements of the law, school personnel are under pressure to minimize costs. That can mean compromising your child's services. (However, do not delay enrolling your child in a program if you don't yet have a private evaluation report: you can always rewrite the IEP later.)

- Visit any classroom recommended for your child. Meet the teachers, aides, therapists, and nurses who work there. Also observe the other children in the class and think about how your child would fit in: for example, if your child is able to imitate and learn from other children, are there other children in the classroom who will be good role models? Or, if you know your child needs intense one-on-one adult attention, are there too few teachers and too many other high-needs children in the classroom to make that possible? Is the room too stimulating for your child? Or too bare? If your child has serious food or environmental allergies or other health concerns, is the classroom safe enough? A classroom that is right for a child of a friend or neighbor may be wrong for yours.

- Visit other classrooms and programs, including any others available in your school district, those in neighboring school districts, and those at private schools, even if you have no intention of sending your child there, to give you a framework for comparison.
- Do your own research before sitting down with school personnel. Read up on special education law and on the best educational practices for children with your child's delays or disabilities. (See the Resources section.)
- And, while you must always be prepared to fight, come to every meeting and start every phone call with a positive attitude (or the best one you can muster). Treat people with respect. Be firm, but friendly. Parents who yell, threaten, and send angry letters may work against their child's best interests.
- Don't make demands, but do learn to negotiate. The school system won't give you two hours of speech therapy a week? Well, maybe they'll give you ninety minutes and agree to revisit the issue in a couple of months. You won't know if you don't ask.
- Make specific suggestions for goals that should be included in your child's IEP. But don't micromanage the process. The quality of the overall program and staff probably are more important than the specific list of goals.
- Insist on appropriate, year-round services for your child. Often, school personnel will argue that what is provided

during the traditional nine-month school year is adequate. Or they will offer brief, often poorly staffed "summer school" programs to children who qualify for much meatier programs during the school year. Don't accept that. If you had a child with impaired hearing, you wouldn't put her hearing aides in a drawer for the summer; likewise a child with poor social and communication skills will not benefit from a "break" in learning. First Signs adviser Catherine Lord, lead author on a 2001 report setting educational standards for children with autism spectrum disorders, says: "Year-round programming is critical for students with ASD. Research has shown that children with autism who have made very significant gains during intensive intervention often lose skills when such interventions are stopped abruptly." A summer program doesn't have to be identical to a school-year program: For example, it might include more outdoor and recreational activities. But it should be fully staffed by teachers and therapists just as qualified as a child's school-year providers.

• Keep notes of every phone call and meeting. Follow up important discussions with letters outlining what was said and what you expect as a next step.

I have a doctorate in special ed. I probably know more about the research and know the best practices better than a lot of school staff. And yet I can still walk into a team meeting and there's a part of me that feels like I'm two feet tall. It still can be a very intimidating experience.

Gail Tino of Massachusetts, mother of Max, an
eighteen-year-old with autism

Dealing with Insurers

When your child has a developmental delay or disorder, your world changes. One of the biggest and most stressful changes is financial: evaluation, diagnosis, and treatment can cost a lot of money. Public Early Intervention programs and school systems may provide their services at no cost to your family, but most children require more than those systems provide. That's why you need to start learning about your health insurance. It may not seem fair, but parents who know what benefits their children are entitled to, and who work hard to get them, get more from their insurers than parents who remain passive.

What you need to do:
- Get the most recent copy of your insurance plan and read it. (If you don't have this at home, look for it at your insurer's website or call the customer service number on the back of your insurance card and request a copy.)
- Make sure you learn the basics—for example, whether your child always needs a referral to see a specialist and whether you will pay more if she sees someone outside the plan's network or at a "nonparticipating" hospital or clinic. Know whether some procedures or therapies need to be preapproved. And find out if there ever are exceptions to these basic rules: for example, some plans will pay for out-of-network specialists if the care you need is not provided by anyone in their network.
- As you read through your plan, look for the language it uses to describe the services your child needs. For example, you may find that the plan covers "occupational therapy," but see nothing about "sensory integration therapy" (which is a specific kind of therapy offered by many occupational therapists). Also, note whether the plan specifically excludes certain diagnoses (such as "developmental delay" or "autism"). Make sure you use the

language in the plan when you talk or correspond with representatives of the insurance company.

- Enlist providers to help get services covered. Many have staff members who will call insurers and specialists to help obtain coverage. These people will know how to describe your child's treatment and his diagnosis in terms understood by your insurer and the professionals involved. They also will know when an alternative but equally valid diagnostic code might make the difference between coverage and denial.

- When you call a customer service line at your insurance company, remember you are talking to a clerk, not a medical expert. Don't get into a complex discussion of your child's condition and treatment options. Stick to the questions you need to ask about coverage and, again, try to use language that is in the written policy.

- If your child's case is complicated, the insurance company will assign a case manager. Talk to this person—who should be a medical professional—rather than a clerk, when at all possible.

- Keep a log of all calls and always get the name of the person you spoke with. Be assured that the insurance company is doing the same. Your records could be important if you need to appeal a decision or correct an error.

- If coverage is denied, you have a right to appeal. Ask your insurer to explain the appeals process to you.

- If you find yourself unable to communicate with a particular insurance company employee—and especially if you are getting angry on the phone—end the call. Call back later and talk with someone else.

- Find out what supplementary health insurance is available for children with disabilities in your state. All states offer Medicaid coverage for people with disabilities, but income cutoffs vary. Some states also offer special health plans for people with disabilities, often through an office of medical assistance.

- If you work for a large corporation, tell the human resources department about your situation and ask whether the company offers any assistance outside of the insurance plan. Some companies have set up special funds to cover certain employee expenses that are not covered by insurance.
- Take advantage of flexible spending accounts—money you can set aside, tax free, from your paycheck and then use to cover medical expenses, including co-payments and deductibles, that are not covered by insurance.
- When you have an opportunity to switch insurers or switch jobs, make sure you know how your child's coverage will be affected and whether you will be able to keep using current providers. You have every right to shop for the best deal.

Despite your best efforts, you may find that some of the treatments you feel are absolutely needed for your child will not be covered by insurance. You may have to redouble efforts to get services included or increased in your child's Early Intervention or school system program. But you may find yourself in a common bind: The same service that is considered educational (and therefore, not covered) by a medical insurer may be considered medical (and therefore, not provided) by a school system. Parents and advocacy groups nationwide are working to improve this situation. In the meantime, many parents will find themselves digging deep into their own pockets.

No matter how prepared you are, this process can be daunting. The first time I went through it with Sarah, when she was three, I made a big mistake: I agreed to put her in a brand-new program that had never been tried or tested. On paper, it looked good. And the assigned teacher seemed knowledgeable. Within just a few weeks, however, I saw that the program was a disaster for Sarah. I would go to observe the class and find her wandering aimlessly around the room, while the teacher dealt with several more severely disabled children. Or I'd find her working on simple puzzles, far below her ability level. Sarah was overwhelmed and underchallenged. Meanwhile, her behavior deteriorated: every day, as soon as she left school, she flew into a severe tantrum. I then did what I should have done earlier: I visited ten different schools and found one thirty minutes away that was a great fit for my daughter. But it took me five months of fighting the school system, day in and day out, to get her into that more appropriate school. I even ended up taking my complaints to the local media. The experience was so bad that I moved to a new school district when it was time for Sarah to be mainstreamed into kindergarten. Today, happily, Sarah's education is a much more collaborative effort.

Ideally, you and the other members of your child's educational team will be able to work together, in a businesslike and collaborative way, from day one. Certainly, you should have some sympathy for school personnel: most of them want to help and are working with limited resources. If you remain clear, positive, and persistent, most will try to work with you. Given the time and expense involved, no one really wants to engage in an all-out battle—not you, not the special education administrators, and certainly not the hardworking teachers and therapists at your child's IEP meetings.

However, if the school system insists on a program that does not meet your child's needs, you will need to fight. That may mean hiring a professional advocate or lawyer. If the changes you wish to make to the program will benefit other children in addition to your own, consider joining forces with several families so you can share the legal expense and maximize the impact. But first contact the special education director for your district to see if something can be worked out to your satisfaction. In some states, the department of education has a special office dedicated to dispute resolution for parents and schools. So learn your rights—and exercise them.

You have to realize that they only have a certain amount of money. Well-informed parents who fight for services will get them. Other parents who are not informed won't get them. It's unfair, but that's the way it is.

Joy Johnson of Maryland, mother of
two boys with autism

On Your Way

And so, bit by bit, you and your child will be on your way. By the time you've visited a specialist or two, started some interventions and made contact with your local Early Intervention program or school system, many of your initial fears may start to diminish. You quickly will see that there is much you can do to help your child. Before you know it, you, too, will be a specialist: a specialist in guiding your child through the maze, toward the healthiest developmental path possible.

To Do Now

You can help others get to know your child quickly if you take the time now to write his life history.

Don't get carried away: no one wants to read a single-spaced, twenty-page epic about a two-year-old. But you can help new doctors, therapists, teachers, and others understand your child if you provide them with more background than a typical intake questionnaire allows.

So write a short profile, detailing your child's health and developmental history, along with the facts about any intervention he's already received. Share what you know about his developmental strengths and vulnerabilities. If your child's story includes dramatic changes—a sudden loss of skills or a reversal in temperament—be sure to include that.

Update your child's profile from time to time. And, whenever you give out a copy, attach an up-to-date photo. That will help busy professionals to remember him, and to keep his needs in mind.

~ Robby's Story

By the time Robby Oberleitner was fifteen months old, his parents knew something was wrong with their third child. Mom Sharon, a homemaker, and dad Ron, an executive with a medical device company, thought the problem might be Robby's hearing. After all, he'd had a lot of ear infections. Maybe that was why he'd stopped saying "Mama," "Dada," and "bye-bye." Maybe that was why he seemed not to notice when a fire engine raced by their Texas home.

Doctors said, "Give him time," Sharon recalls. "It wasn't serious." But soon, Robby stopped using words altogether. To communicate, he screamed and cried. Sometimes he would grab his mother's hair and pull her to her knees. When visitors came, he would flee up the stairs and hide under his crib.

Sharon kept asking doctors what might be wrong. "It was always taken very lightly," she says. The doctors agreed Robby might be "a little behind," Sharon says, but did not recommend any testing. "They probably thought I was a neurotic mother."

And then, one day, Sharon dropped Robby off for a neighborhood play group. She returned to find him "out of control, screaming." Another mother said Robby seemed deaf. That suggestion might have shocked or offended some parents. But Sharon and Ron were relieved to hear that someone else knew that Robby was not okay, that he needed help. By then, they were hoping he was deaf. "I was thinking, I'll learn sign language. We'll take care of this," Sharon says. She made an appointment for a hearing test. And it showed nothing.

But now, Sharon and Ron knew they needed answers. Increasingly afraid of what they might learn, the couple had Robby evaluated by an Early Intervention team. The professionals spent hours testing the two-year-old—and came back with answers that only baffled his parents. They said he was "gravitationally insecure," that he "didn't know where his body was in space and time," Sharon recalls. The prescribed therapy: a couple of hours weekly with a teacher who came to the family's home. The teacher came regularly, but Robby just got worse. "He was hyperactive. He couldn't sit in a chair. He was aggressive. He would scratch, pull hair, kick," Sharon says.

Meanwhile, Ron had started reading about autism. And much of what he read seemed to fit Robby. But Sharon thought the idea was ridiculous: "I thought an autistic child would just sit in a corner, rock and bang his head against the wall." She was angry at Ron for suggesting the notion. And Ron didn't want to push his view: after all, he had no idea what they'd do differently if Robby had autism.

Around the time Robby turned three, the family moved to New Jersey. At his first preschool there—a public program for children with disabilities—teachers strapped Robby in his chair for hours at a time, saying it was the only way they could teach the increasingly aggressive boy. Sharon cringed every time she saw him at that school, strapped to his chair, idly watching the colorful toys his teachers placed before him while they worked with other, less challenging children. Robby was learning nothing.

Distraught, Sharon turned to the school's psychologist, demanding answers. He handed her a take-home questionnaire from a diagnostic test called the Childhood Autism Rating Scale (CARS). Again, Sharon saw the word *autism* and scoffed. Her picture of autism did not match her picture of Robby. "And tly," she says, "I just didn't want to believe it." Then she read the questions. Halfway through, "I knew he had autism," she says.

Robby was three and a half. His parents had spent a year and a half trying to put a name to his differences—and, they believe now, had wasted precious time on ineffective therapies.

"That's when our whole world changed," Sharon says. "We started using techniques that worked." Within a short time, Robby was formally diagnosed with autism. Armed with that diagnosis, his parents demanded that his school hire someone who knew how to teach children with autism. And the school agreed. With a new teacher in charge, Robby began receiving an intense form of therapy called applied behavioral analysis (ABA), which involves teaching skills in small steps, with a great deal of repetition and constant reward.

"The first thing they taught him was to sit," Sharon says. Robby's progress was slow, his gains incremental, but he was never strapped to a chair again. Eventually, he learned to work willingly with therapists and teachers, both at home and at school. Therapists also taught Sharon and Ron how to improve Robby's behavior in public so that they could take him to restaurants and grocery stores. Bit by bit, life for the whole family got a little better, a little more normal.

Over the years, Robby has continued to make slow progress. At age eleven, he uses a few words and can spell and do some reading and basic math. Sometimes, he uses a special computer to communicate. In fact, he's something of a computer whiz. "He can figure out passwords and reprogram things," Sharon says. And recently, he has developed a passion for river rafting. All in all, his parents says, he is a happy boy.

Life for the Oberleitners hasn't been easy, though. Robby has been through several schools and many therapies, and his care has often been expensive. To make ends meet, the family recently moved again, to Idaho. And they still are trying new therapies for Robby, trying to prepare him for the most independent life possible.

Ron and Sharon have become advocates for early recognition and diagnosis of autism spectrum disorders, often sharing their experiences with other parents. "We really feel the pain that we didn't get Robby off to a quick start with his education," Ron says. Sharon says: "I definitely, firmly believe that the earlier you get it, the better off you are."

Chapter Six
Diagnosis

The silent, sleepy-eyed boy munching dry Cheerios at your breakfast table is not "autism" or an "expressive language disorder." The giggling girl running circles around your sofa is not "sensory integration dysfunction" or "ADHD." Your child is a child, with unique strengths and weaknesses, a personality, a life history, and a family. You could raise, love, and nurture that child without ever having him formally diagnosed.

But I don't recommend it. While your child always will be Danny or Claire or Alex to you, he or she may need to become a case of "PDD" or "OCD" or "fragile X" to get what you need from insurers and service providers, bureaucracies that base their rules on specific diagnostic and procedural codes. If you don't attach the appropriate codes to your child—if you don't have him properly, formally diagnosed—you risk not getting him the help he needs, or bankrupting yourself paying for it.

Don't look at the process of formal diagnosis as only an exercise in bureaucratic labeling. Ideally, it also will be an opportunity for you and the professionals who work with your child to deepen your understanding of his unique developmental profile. It's not enough, for example, to know that a child has Asperger syndrome. That only tells you that he is a child with adequate language and intelligence who nonetheless has limited interests and some serious social and communication problems. It does not tell you whether he has an excellent memory or a poor one, whether he learns best through looking or listening, or whether he has good or poor control of his muscles, much less whether he's a child whose whole day can be ruined by a hole in his sock or too much milk. A good diagnostic workup will answer many questions and give you vital clues about how to help.

Enter the diagnostic process resigned to the fact your child may end up with a label or two, but focused on finding the information you need to improve your child's life.

Diagnosis Makes a Difference

By now, you've set up some initial appointments for your child. You may have seen some specialists and started talking with them about what your child's diagnosis might be. But you need more.

You need at least one thorough, independent evaluation report, containing a diagnosis—if one is warranted—that you can take to your Early Intervention program or school system. You don't need to get this report before you enroll your child in a program. It's much more important to get her started with services. But you should not rely, long term, on the evaluations you get from Early Intervention or school system personnel. Remember:

- Early Intervention programs and school systems may label children—often in the vaguest possible terms—but do not diagnose them.
- The people who evaluate children for Early Intervention and school special education services have varying levels of skill: some are very good at what they do, and some are not.
- Despite legal requirements to provide appropriate services and despite the good intentions of most of the people involved, these agencies and school systems are under pressure to minimize costs by minimizing services.

The differences in the services provided to children with and without a diagnosis can be huge. In some states, a toddler labeled with "language and fine motor delays" or even "global developmental delays" might get nothing more than an hour of speech therapy and an hour of occupational therapy each week. The same child diagnosed with autism might qualify for thirty to forty hours of intense, one-on-one play or behavioral therapy, as well as speech and occupational therapy. In other states, no diagnosis will elicit such a high level of service, though having the diagnosis may make the difference if you pursue legal action. Of course, a diagnosis also will help determine what your health insurer will cover. It also will guide you toward the specific information, treatments, and services best suited for your child.

> I told the doctors, "I want you to name it. Because if it doesn't have a name, I can't get the services I need." Everyone was very hesitant to make a diagnosis at such a young age, but I insisted.
>
> *Debra Egan of New Jersey, mother of Gabi,*
> *diagnosed with autism at eighteen months*

There's one more thing: a diagnosis can help others understand your child's difficulties. A diagnosis doesn't define your child, but it can be a shorthand way to let others know about her challenges—and about yours. In Sarah's case, it's often been in her best interest for relatives, camp counselors, babysitters, and other adults—beyond doctors and teachers—to know about her special needs. And for me, sharing my concerns about Sarah with family members, friends, and other parents of children with developmental challenges, has been a great source of comfort and support. I've found that most people want to know what we are going through and want to help. Sometimes that means just listening to me or offering a kind word when I'm down. Sometimes it means more practical help, especially from parents in the same boat, who almost always are eager to share their own stories and tips.

Deciding whom to tell about your own child's diagnosis is a highly personal matter. You are under no obligation to tell anyone, unless, of course, not doing so would endanger your child. I heard of one family who learned that their five-year-old twins had fragile X syndrome, a genetic disorder that causes widely varying degrees of mental impairment. But the two children, a boy and a girl, were not nearly as disabled as the individuals with fragile X whom the distraught parents first read about in some outdated medical journals. Their daughter, in particular, had only mild delays. So they made a decision: they would tell no one at the children's school about the diagnosis. They were terrified that expectations for both children would plummet if they did. Within a few months, after the parents had learned more, they decided to inform their son's teachers. But they waited years—until their fifth-grade daughter was struggling with apparent learning disabilities—to disclose her diagnosis as well.

Some families decide to share a diagnosis with doctors, therapists, and teachers, but no one else. Often they worry about the stigma that might be attached to their child's disorder. One mother of a boy with autism said: "I didn't want to tell anyone because I was afraid he wouldn't get a date for the prom." (Her son was three at the time.)

In deciding whether to inform professionals—educators, insurers, and health care workers—bear in mind that laws protect your child's privacy. None of these professionals may talk about your child with anyone, not even each other, without your written permission.

Getting the Diagnosis: Where to Start

If a teacher or occupational therapist or your best friend has told you that your child has "attention deficit disorder" or "autism" or an "emotional disorder," you have one person's opinion. It may be right or wrong, well informed or poorly informed, but it is not a diagnosis. Likewise, most teachers, therapists, and friends are qualified to make medical diagnoses. (Though some therapists diagnose or rule out a narrow range of conditions in which they specialize, such as speech impediments or fine motor delays.)

The speech therapist would be coming to my house every week. And I'd ask, "What do you think? Do you think it's autism?" She didn't really know. But she said, "Oh, I would be really shocked if he ever got the diagnosis of autism." So I asked, "What would you do if it was your kid?" She said, "Well, if it was my kid I would get him evaluated." That was really good advice.

Mary Barbera of Pennsylvania, mother of Lucas,
diagnosed with autism at age three

To get a diagnosis, you need to go to someone who is qualified to give it—either a medical doctor or a highly specialized psychologist who is experienced in diagnosing children with disorders of communicating, relating, and behavior. This expert can't just be any doctor or psychologist. Not all pediatricians or pediatric neurologists are experts in child development; not all developmental psychologists know how to evaluate babies and toddlers or are experienced enough to recognize a child with a rare condition. Missed diagnoses and misdiagnoses are extremely common among young children with complex developmental disorders. Check each specialist's credentials before you make an appointment, so you don't waste precious time going in the wrong direction. If you and your pediatrician still aren't sure whom your child should see, start with a good developmental pediatrician. She should be able to point you the right way.

At your initial appointment with any specialist, make it clear that you want your child to be thoroughly evaluated and diagnosed. Don't settle for an informal opinion. And don't accept any version of "Wait and see," such as "Well, it could be a PDD, but as long as you've got her in a good preschool program and speech therapy, I don't see any reason to label her right now." The whole point is that you want a complete evaluation—and any diagnosis that arises from it—so that you can assess whether you are doing the right things to help your child.

What kind of evaluation do you need? Initial screening and observations of your child, along with his developmental history, will provide some clues. Certainly, children with apparent speech delays need full speech and language evaluations; those with significant motor delays need to be assessed by both physicians and occupational or physical therapists. But parents and pediatricians often don't realize the full extent or nature of a child's delays. So most of the children we're discussing—children who have problems with communication, social-emotional skills, or behavior—need an even more thorough assessment, one that allows parents and professionals to sort through what is usually a complex medical and developmental picture.

The Multidisciplinary Evaluation

The gold standard of diagnosis for such children is the multidisciplinary evaluation (MDE). Simply put, this means the child should be evaluated by a team of professionals from several different specialties. Often, this will include

- at least one physician, such as a neurologist, psychiatrist, or developmental pediatrician
- a psychologist specializing in child development
- a speech-language pathologist
- an occupational and/or physical therapist
- a special educator
- a social worker

And the evaluation will include several different kinds of assessments, often including

- formal testing of a child's cognitive, language, and motor skills. These tests vary, depending on the child's age and developmental stage, but might include working with puzzles, blocks and other toys, using crayons, and following simple directions.

- observations of the child's communication, social, and play skills. An evaluator might watch you play with your child and then try to engage the child herself.
- parent interviews and questionnaires. You will be asked about your child's health and development, your concerns and priorities, and your family's lifestyle and support system.
- physical exams, blood tests, and other medical tests, sometimes including brain scans.

These tests, interviews, and observations might all be done at the same place and time, over one or two very long days, or might take place during several appointments at different places. In either case, at the end of the process, one team member will collect all the information and assemble a complete evaluation report.

So where can you get an MDE? For most families just starting out, the best bet is to find a good regional child-development center. These often are affiliated with major children's hospitals. If you suspect an autism spectrum disorder, it's also worth looking for a child-development clinic that specializes in diagnosing and treating these disorders. There also are clinics that specialize in particular genetic disorders, mental health disorders, and so on. It can be worth your time and money to seek out such specialized attention. It's always worth the effort to check out the credentials and expertise of the professionals and the facility you are considering for this important job. The closest clinic may not be the best one, so don't hesitate to shop around.

It also is possible to put together your own MDE team, using professionals who already know your child or who you know are particularly well qualified to assess her. I have done this for Sarah, but hesitate to recommend such a big assignment for parents just starting out. It can take months to coordinate the schedules of several busy professionals.

So, for most families, the MDE will start with a phone call to a child-development center. Don't be surprised to hear that the wait for appointments is three months, six months, a year, or more. Just get on the waiting list and go from there. Once your child has a diagnosis and starts treatment, you'll want to repeat some version of the MDE every two or three years—in no small part because you will always want an up-to-date assessment to share with school officials, new doctors, and others. So get in the habit now of making appointments well in advance.

How to Prepare

As the big testing day or days approach, you can do much to prepare.

- Get the schedule in advance and make sure that you and your child have time for snacks, lunch, and other breaks. Look for pitfalls. If there's just too much packed into one day, speak up and ask for the appointments to be spread over two days or more. And don't allow your child to start the day with an anxiety-provoking blood test if it could just as well be done at the end of the day or on another day entirely. I made that mistake once with Sarah: she cried for an hour after the blood test, then fell asleep, wasting the time of a very annoyed neurologist.
- Learn who will be part of the evaluation team. If you know someone on the team is a bad fit—say a speech therapist who saw your child in the past and seemed unable to engage her as well as other professionals—you may be able to make a change.
- Learn exactly what will be expected of your child during the workup. Will she have a chance to play with toys? Look at books? Will she be wearing earphones, working with a "teacher," being weighed and measured? The more you know, the better you can prepare her. Depending on

her needs and developmental age, this might mean telling her stories or showing her pictures of what to expect; it could mean speaking with team members in advance to explain what activities might require extra time for your child or how they might distract her during a procedure she's likely to find painful or scary.

- Get any forms you need and fill them out in advance. This is crucial for any questionnaires about your child's health and development. Take the time to answer these questions as thoroughly and as accurately as possible.

- Do a little personal research. Go back through your child's baby books and videos and look at your diary or at notes from child care providers to document developmental progress, focusing on milestones met and missed. "Interview" grandparents, nannies, and preschool teachers to refresh and supplement your own memory. If anyone seems to have special insight, ask them to write a letter about your child for the evaluation team.

- In the two weeks leading up to the evaluation, keep a detailed diary recording your child's key behaviors (eye contact, inappropriate play or behavior, not responding to his name, anxieties, moods, odd or repetitive body movements or mannerisms); sleep patterns (note if your child is having difficulty falling asleep, how many times a night he wakes up, if his sleep is peaceful or fitful); diet (note if your child is a picky eater or has rigid food preferences, types of foods your child is eating and how often, changes in behavior after eating those foods); physiology (ear or sinus infections, frequency and consistency of bowel movements, stomach aches, reflux, dark circles under eyes, red ears, rashes on face or body), and so on, summarizing your concerns.

- Assemble all your child's medical records and prepare copies to leave with the team.

- Pack a bag with toys, books, snacks, or anything that might comfort or amuse your child during a long wait or an unpleasant procedure. Be sure to include some new items or small treats you can use to reward her for cooperative behavior. If you will be away all day, pack a lunch.
- Bring a notebook and pen to record your observations and key comments from team members.

Getting Results

During your child's assessment, feel free to ask questions. Many professionals will share their initial impressions—and even give you some tips for helping your child—while they are in the process of evaluating him. Getting this verbal feedback is good, but, if possible, avoid having a detailed discussion about the likely diagnosis while your child is in the room, no matter what you think his level of understanding may be. And don't expect to leave a multidisciplinary evaluation with a written diagnosis and treatment plan in hand. Instead, expect to wait a few weeks for the team's final report.

Insist on getting this report during an in-person follow-up appointment, preferably at a time when you can come with another adult but without your child. If at all possible, both parents should come to this crucial appointment. After all, this may be the first time that you get solid, complete information about the extent of your child's problems. This is not the kind of information you want to get alone, over the phone, or while entertaining a bored, cranky child. Ideally, the lead evaluator will take time to explain the findings to you before letting you read the black-and-white report—often a gut-wrenching experience.

What will this document contain? Typically, such reports have several kinds of information:

- formal scores on tests of cognition, speech, motor, social-emotional, and self-help skills. These scores may be expressed as ages (for example, you may read that your two-year-old has the social skills of a typical ten-month-old) or as numbers (you may read that the same two-year-old scored a 70 on a measure of cognitive development in which the average score is 100).

- detailed descriptions of team members' observations and concerns, focusing on findings that illuminate the child's strengths and weaknesses.
- a diagnosis—or more than one diagnosis—if any can be determined.
- recommendations for intervention. These should include referrals for particular services and treatments, as well as detailed suggestions on how parents can help their child at home.

Amid all this information, many parents tend to focus on two things: the diagnosis and the numbers, especially scary numbers that quantify just how far behind a child may be in some areas of development. But, remember, your child still is your child: he or she is not the diagnosis. And that diagnosis is going to help you get your child the help he or she needs. As for the numbers: as concrete as they may look, they are nothing more than a snapshot of how your young child performed on one day, on one test or set of tests. For an infant, toddler, or young preschooler, any one score tells you very little about how that child is likely to perform on similar tests—whether they are IQ tests or academic tests or language measures—years down the road. Sarah's first full evaluation included a cognitive score well below her age level, something that crushed me at the time, but that turned out to have no relation to her actual intelligence. Sometimes a low score just means that the person administering the test was unable to get your child to pay attention and cooperate enough to show his true potential. (A skilled evaluator will acknowledge this in the report. It's also something you should watch out for and take note of during the testing.) Sometimes it means that some other problem the child has—say, processing what she hears, or planning her actions—got in the way of performing the assigned task (say, stacking four blocks or following a two-step command). And sometimes a low score does mean that the child has a real weakness in the area tested and needs a lot of help. Put your focus on getting that help, and on recognizing and building upon your child's strengths.

If you get a report that confuses you, ask questions until it makes sense. If there isn't enough information, especially on the next steps you should take, insist on getting more. And don't be afraid to ask the evaluators if they can endorse a plan of action—say, a particular classroom placement or type of therapy—that you think will help. If they agree that your child should be in a classroom that happens to be outside your school system, or that she should get an intense home-therapy program that neither your Early Intervention program nor your insurer wants to fund, get that opinion in writing.

Finally, if any report you get about your child, from a team or an individual specialist, just seems wrong—if it describes a child you don't recognize—trust your instincts. Although it may seem daunting, seeking yet another opinion, from a different specialist or team, may be necessary to get your child the right help.

My son was first evaluated by a developmental pediatrician. He put "PDD" in the report, but he didn't explain what it meant. He didn't really want to diagnose him; he kind of sidestepped it. Later we saw a psychologist who diagnosed my son with oppositional defiant disorder. After he handed that to me, I said, "Do you realize how wrong you are?" He was saying my son was oppositional because he wouldn't sit in the chair and work with him. He was crawling under the chair, looking at something else, but he wasn't even understanding what the guy was saying. Finally, we found another psychologist. She said, "I have no problem giving you this diagnosis. But I have to be honest. Usually I have to break this news. Very rarely do I have someone asking for it." I said, "Well, I have mixed emotions. Obviously I don't want you to be telling me this, but now I can go get what I need for services." So finally, at three he was diagnosed with autism.

Brenda Eaton of Pennsylvania, mother of Brendan,
diagnosed with autism at age three

More Than One Diagnosis

Many parents start this process with the idea, the hope, that their child's problems, no matter how varied, can be explained with one name—and, ideally, addressed with one "magic bullet" therapy. In fact, though, many a child with developmental problems gets more than one diagnosis. Often, this is because the child has numerous, related problems. Sometimes it's because he is inaccurately diagnosed at first and later gets a more appropriate diagnosis. Sometimes, his underlying problems manifest themselves in one way early on (say, with language delay in toddlerhood) and another way later (with inattention or poor impulse control in early school years), a course to different but equally valid diagnoses. And sometimes it's a matter of perspective: what looks like "autism" to a neuropsychologist looks like "sensory integration disorder" to an occupational therapist and "expressive language disorder" to a speech therapist. Every one of them may be right—and each may have excellent, though differing, ideas about how to address the same child's problems.

For parents, the important thing is to realize that children can have these "overlapping diagnoses" or can develop new problems over time. Learning that your child has one particular disorder should never blind you—or your child's doctors, teachers, and therapists—to the possibility that he may have other important problems as well.

One couple I know has a son who had severe seizures and developmental delays as a baby and toddler. They were told that he had an 85 percent chance of becoming mentally retarded. Hoping for the best, they put him in an Early Intervention program and then a special education preschool. Evaluators from these agencies and a local children's hospital followed this little boy and, at first, said that he seemed to be catching up. His vocabulary growth was particularly striking: he had sixty words at eighteen months and lots of two-word phrases at age two. His parents were perplexed and alarmed, then, when the little boy stopped learning any new language around age three. He also began chewing his shirts, screaming, flapping his hands, and throwing intense tantrums for no apparent reason. The child's neurologist said he was now clearly showing signs of mental retardation.

Only then did his parents start to focus on other facts—for example, the child had never used gestures, never engaged in pretend play, never imitated other children, and, most strikingly, had never used his good vocabulary to engage in real back-and-forth conversation. In fact, the boy had autism, something that his teachers and doctors had overlooked while treating his seizures and more broadly defined "developmental delays." The parents had their little boy moved to a classroom where he would get more individual teaching of basic social, communication, and play skills; they also hired therapists to work with him at home. He quickly began to make progress.

Today, the boy is in first grade. He still has problems with conversation and spends part of each day flapping his hands and screaming. But he also speaks in complex sentences, imitates his big brother, enjoys studying maps, and can read and write as well as any seven-year-old. His latest breakthrough is that he can take a spelling test with his classmates without blurting out the (correct) answer to everyone in the room. He still has autism but is clearly not retarded.

Another family was initially told that their two-year-old twins, a boy and a girl, had speech delays. At age four, the boy was diagnosed with "PDD." Only when the children were five did doctors—nudged by a perceptive speech therapist—perform a simple blood test that revealed both children had fragile X, a genetic syndrome.

Yet another family had triplet boys. Two were diagnosed with autism and one with a language disorder at age three. A year later, testing showed that one boy did not have autism at all: he was, rather, hearing impaired. Once he got hearing aids, his apparently autistic behaviors, including a rigid insistence on routine, disappeared. Meanwhile, doctors decided that the brother originally diagnosed with a language disorder really did have autism, a label later changed to Asperger syndrome.

In another heart-wrenching case, a boy who had struggled to get along with other children since toddlerhood—and who had been labeled emotionally disturbed by school personnel—fell into a deep depression at age eight. He was being hit and harassed at school and told his parents that he was "nothing." His mood darkened so severely that he had to be hospitalized for two weeks. Only then did a team of psychiatrists figure out his underlying problem: he had Asperger syndrome, and his very poor social and communication skills were making it impossible for him to navigate the world of other children. His mother says: "My husband and I felt so unbelievably relieved. We felt like we could now help him. We said, 'Thank you, God.' "

Sarah's Diagnoses

My own journey with Sarah has taken many twists and turns. Her initial diagnosis, made at twenty-eight months, was PDD-NOS, pervasive developmental disorder–not otherwise specified. She was clearly on the autism spectrum. Karen Levine, the Boston developmental psychologist who diagnosed her (and whose diagnosis was later confirmed by a multidisciplinary evaluation), remembers meeting her the first time: "Sarah mainly danced around the room. . . . She had classic signs. She didn't point. She didn't have any gestures. She didn't have symbolic play."

Karen did notice that, occasionally, Sarah would glance up at me or my mother. That was a good sign. Then, she saw another good sign. She recalls: "We have this mat that's different-colored stripes and she was skipping along it and I started naming the colors and she kind of stopped and looked up. I could tell that she knew the colors. That was our first little connection and that also told me how smart she was." Sarah was reachable. Sarah was smart. And, sure enough, over time and with a lot of intervention, Sarah showed fewer and fewer of those classic signs.

Then, new problems appeared. Overnight, her sweet, calm disposition melted away; suddenly she was having long, intense temper tantrums. I'll never forget the day she had a ninety-minute meltdown in the driveway while I tried, in vain, to coax her inside: I'll bet the neighbors remember it, too. And then there was the two-hour marathon of screaming and crying we endured on one particular plane trip: I'll bet the other passengers recall that one. At the same time, her hyperactivity turned into mania. A tendency to overfocus on a favorite topic became a series of obsessions. My beautiful daughter was diagnosed with ADHD, childhood bipolar disorder, multiple food allergies, and colitis, all before turning six. A few times, she even had clusters of mild seizures. At age eight, with her rages increasingly out of control, additional testing led us to yet another diagnosis: pediatric autoimmune neuropsychiatric disorder associated with streptococcal infections (PANDAS)—meaning that one or more strep infections had triggered an autoimmune attack on her brain. Some researchers theorize that a subset of children with various diagnoses, especially obsessive-compulsive disorder and tics, and possibly autism spectrum disorders, bipolar disorder, and ADHD, may have this underlying problem. In Sarah's case, we still are sorting it all out and trying new treatments. I strongly believe that Sarah's various difficulties are connected by one or more common biological threads. A cascade of immunological and neurological damage triggered by one little bacterial infection could be the key thread.

In any case, over the years, Sarah has had a lot of diagnoses—but she has always been my wonderful, exuberant, spirited little girl. She has never *been* a label or a cluster of disorders. The labels have helped me, though, to find the best treatments for her—treatments that have included everything from medication and special diets to vitamins and supplements to special listening therapies and, most important, intense one-on-one engagement in the world of language, play, and human connection. And as a result, over time, some of her labels have become obsolete: it's often suggested to me today that Sarah—a warm, empathetic, incredibly talkative child—was misdiagnosed with an autism spectrum disorder those years ago. But Sarah was properly diagnosed. The changes in her were made possible because, as a direct result of that diagnosis, she got the early, intense help she needed.

What About Genetics?

Around the time a young child is diagnosed with any developmental disorder, a question often arises: What caused it? Was it something environmental? Or something genetic? Sometimes the answer is clear: certain disorders—fragile X syndrome, Down syndrome, tuberous sclerosis—are the direct result of abnormalities in genes or chromosomes. When children are diagnosed with these disorders, parents must get thorough genetic counseling to let them know how other family members, including future children, might be affected.

Other disorders—such as traumatic brain injury (caused by accident or abuse) or reactive attachment disorder (linked to early abuse and neglect)—are, by definition, the result of environmental factors. But for many more disorders, including autism spectrum disorders, obsessive-compulsive disorder, bipolar disorder, and ADHD—the answer is not so clear. Scientists are certain that genes play important roles in these disorders. But they don't know which genes are involved or in what way. They suspect that certain environmental factors—including infections or exposures to toxins, either in the womb or after birth—might help to trigger some of these disorders in genetically susceptible individuals. Others suspect vaccines or certain foods as triggers, though those are more controversial ideas. Completely rejected is the idea that cold, indifferent parents—the "refrigerator mothers" of 1950s psychoanalysis—somehow cause autism.

In any case, as of the early twenty-first century, the one thing that won't be a part of your child's workup for an autism spectrum disorder, or for most other emotional or behavioral disorders, is a blood test that confirms the diagnosis by finding a particular gene mutation. Researchers hope that such gene tests will exist someday. They also are working to develop other kinds of tests that will pinpoint specific biological differences, in the immune system or elsewhere, that are common in children who are genetically vulnerable to autism and other developmental disorders. The ultimate goal is to develop tests for babies that will not only indicate a high risk for certain disorders but also provide biological profiles that point toward particular treatments. So one child, at high risk for "autism type A," might get preventative play and sensory therapy, while another, at high risk for "autism type B," might immediately be put on a special diet and vitamin regimen.

In the meantime, it's worth thinking about the likelihood that your child's disorder has genetic underpinnings. You can start by looking at yourself. Do you share some of your child's atypical traits? More than one parent has had a moment of recognition when their child was diagnosed with one of these disorders. They suddenly start to think about the fact that they, too, have trouble making friends or tend to obsess on a favorite topic. Some are even motivated to seek treatment for their own difficulties with social skills or emotional regulation.

For most parents, though, the biggest concern is for other children in the family, born and unborn. And the concern is warranted. In the case of autism, for example, studies suggest that if one child is affected, there's a 5 to 10 percent chance that any sibling will have autism and a 30 to 40 percent chance that the sibling will have milder, but related problems. So once one child is diagnosed, it's a good idea to look at siblings and watch for warning signs. Thanks to alert parents and doctors, many affected siblings are now getting the earliest possible diagnosis and treatment.

It's not always younger siblings who are picked up this way; I heard about one mother who took her three-year-old son for a multidisciplinary evaluation—and left with an autism spectrum diagnosis for both him and his six-year-old brother. Alert staffers had noticed warning signs in the older boy while he played with other children in the waiting room.

Embracing the Diagnosis

So, now you know. Your child has a problem, and that problem has a name. You may be devastated. Your hopes and dreams for your child may seem shattered the moment you see that diagnosis in black and white. Your world may seem to end the first time you hear a doctor say "autism" or "mental disorder" or "genetic abnormality." You may grieve for the loss of your imagined, ideal child. Suddenly, every playground and play group, every grocery store and library, may seem full of other people's healthy, thriving children. And you may find yourself gripped with anger at the unfairness of it all. Why your child? Why you? Some people stay sad and angry for a very long time.

> The discovery that our son had a serious mental health disorder struck me as a death in the family. The grieving process was long and severe. Going through the stages of denial, hopelessness, blame, depression, and ultimately acceptance and recovery took nearly three years.
>
> *Fred Wayne of Delaware, father of Derrick,*
> *diagnosed at age three with childhood*
> *bipolar disorder, ADHD, and anxiety*

After we got the diagnosis, our son fell asleep in the car and when we got home, we put him down for a nap. We collapsed—me, six months pregnant, on the couch, and my husband on the floor. We were numb and didn't speak for a very long time. I felt like the child upstairs was someone new and when he woke he would be a different child. A part of me didn't want him to wake up for a while, because then it would be real and I would be expected to carry out new duties I was not equipped or prepared for. He must have known, because he slept all afternoon and into the evening.

Susan Sutherland of Massachusetts, mother of Evan,
diagnosed with PDD-NOS just before age three

For a lot of parents, the moment of truth is also a moment of great relief. You've known for a long time that something was wrong. Now you know what it is. Now you can start to do something about it.

When I finally got Sarah's diagnosis, it was a knife through my heart. I was hurt and numb at the same time. But I knew that I could not curl up and nurse my wounds. Instead, I had to do something, both for Sarah's future and for my own survival. I wasn't going to let anyone or anything take my daughter away from me. And autism was starting to do just that. So I could not turn my back on that awful diagnosis. Instead, I accepted it, embraced it—and set out to fight it.

What the Diagnosis Might Be

Young children with social, emotional, or communication delays and disorders can end up with literally dozens of different diagnoses. These can include disorders that are on the autism spectrum, what are officially known as pervasive developmental disorders (PDDs). The most common of these are:

Autistic Disorder (also known as classic autism, or just autism). Children with autism have impaired speech, social and communication skills, limited interests, and repetitive behaviors (which can include a rigid adherence to daily routines, ritualized, unimaginative play, and so-called "self-stimulating" behaviors like frequent hand-flapping). Some—though probably fewer than once believed—are mentally retarded.

Asperger Syndrome. These children develop speech at a typical age and pace and are often very intelligent, but exhibit markedly impaired social and communication skills. So they may do a lot of talking, but have problems keeping up a conversation, reading gestures and facial expressions, and understanding basic social rules. They also have narrow interests—often becoming obsessed with a single topic for months or years—and engage in rigid, repetitive behaviors.

Pervasive Developmental Disorder–not otherwise specified. Technically, this diagnosis should be reserved for children who show some signs of an autism spectrum disorder but do not fully qualify for a more specific diagnosis, either because impairments are too mild or because some important signs are missing. In practice, doctors commonly give this label to children under age three who show any signs of autism, often because they don't yet know how severely affected the child is. Children diagnosed with PDD-NOS at an early age often are later diagnosed with autistic disorder or Asperger syndrome; others retain the PDD-NOS diagnosis or fall off the autism spectrum altogether.

Two other much rarer conditions are considered pervasive developmental disorders:

Rett Syndrome. This genetic disorder affects mostly girls. The children develop typically for six to eighteen months, then lose communication and social skills along with purposeful use of their hands. Repetitive hand movements arise; seizures are common.

Childhood Disintegrative Disorder. Children with this disorder develop typically for an even longer period, usually two to four years, then lose language, social, and self-help skills. Most become severely disabled.

Many other disorders involve delays in communication, social skills, or both, along with behavioral difficulties. These include several that often accompany an autism spectrum disorder, but also can be found in children without autism.

Sensory Integration Dysfunction. An inability of the brain to correctly process information from the senses. Children may seem undersensitive (for example, they may show little reaction to pain or noise); oversensitive (they may be unable to tolerate shirt labels, loud voices, bright lights); or, often, both.

Auditory Processing Disorder. The child has a normal ability to hear sounds, but trouble interpreting what he hears. Problems can be especially severe in loud environments or in situations where complex information is relayed through speech, such as classrooms.

Expressive Language Disorder. Children with this disorder often speak late, then have limited vocabularies and trouble recalling words and producing complex or lengthy sentences.

Speech Apraxia. A speech delay caused by a breakdown in communication between the brain and the muscles involved in speech. Children with severe speech apraxia may not speak at all or may be very difficult to understand, but they know what they want to say.

Attention Deficit Hyperactivity Disorder (ADHD). This common disorder is characterized by poor attention skills, impulsive behavior, and a high level of activity, including, for example, constant fidgeting, aimless running, and difficulty sitting still for meals and lessons.

Attention Deficit Disorder (ADD). This disorder resembles ADHD, minus the high level of activity.

Mental Retardation. Significantly below average general intelligence (usually defined as an IQ of 70 or lower), coupled with difficulties with daily activities such as toilet training and eating skills.

Other diagnoses often considered include:

Hearing Impairment. A reduced or absent ability to hear sounds. This can profoundly affect a child's social and communication skills and lead to disruptive behaviors.

Seizure Disorders. Infantile spasms (clusters of seizures seen in babies and toddlers) and Landau-Kleffner syndrome (characterized

by abnormal brainwaves and, often, nighttime seizures) are among disorders that can cause a delay or loss of social and communication skills in young children.

Nonverbal Learning Disorder. Children with this disorder speak fluently and easily remember what they hear, but have trouble with social skills and abstract thinking. They also tend to be physically awkward and anxious about changes in routine.

Traumatic Brain Injury. Children whose impairments in thinking, language, social skills, and behavior can be linked to a particular brain injury—caused by accident, insufficient oxygen, poisoning, or infection—may receive this diagnosis.

In addition, doctors sometimes test children for certain genetic conditions that can mimic or share characteristics with autism spectrum disorders:

Fragile X Syndrome. This is the most common, known inherited cause of both mental retardation and autism. However, not all children with fragile X have autism, and few children with autism turn out to have fragile X.

Tuberous Sclerosis. This complex condition is characterized by lesions that grow on the skin, the brain, and other organs. Seizures are common. Autism and mental retardation develop in some, but not all, children with the condition.

Williams Syndrome. Children with this syndrome usually are quite talkative and eager for social interaction, but can also be inattentive, anxious, and prone to socially inappropriate behaviors. They also have physical health problems.

Angelman Syndrome. This condition usually causes severe mental retardation, a lack of speech, and tremors and other movement problems. Seizures are common, as are frequent, unexplained laughter or smiling.

Prader-Willi Syndrome. The first signs are developmental delays and feeding problems in infancy. After age one, the children begin a pattern of compulsive eating, food obsessions, and obesity.

Phenylketonuria. This metabolic disorder, which can be de-

tected at birth, causes mental retardation and organ damage unless controlled with a special diet early in life.

Finally, for some children, doctors consider certain psychiatric conditions.

Early-Onset Childhood Bipolar Disorder. Once known as manic-depression, this condition is increasingly recognized in young children. Signs include extreme, frequent changes in mood, energy, thinking, and behavior. Rages are common.

Generalized Anxiety Disorder. Children who display excessive worrying, restlessness, and fears may get this diagnosis.

Obsessive-Compulsive Disorder. In this disorder, a child's daily life is disrupted by unwanted, repetitive thoughts and an overwhelming need to repeat certain rituals. For example, the child may need to do ten things in a particular order before he can walk out the door, or may need to wash his hands dozens of times a day.

Selective Mutism. Children who speak normally in some settings, but are silent in others—often school or other socially demanding settings—may be diagnosed with this anxiety disorder.

Pediatric Autoimmune Neuropsychiatric Disorders Associated with Streptococcal Infections (PANDAS). In this still poorly understood disorder, infections with strep bacteria trigger an immune attack on the child's central nervous system, causing problems with behavior, thinking, and, sometimes, movement.

Oppositional Defiant Disorder. Children with this disorder are uncooperative, defiant, and hostile toward parents and other authority figures.

Reactive Attachment Disorder. Often diagnosed in children who have been neglected or abused, this disorder is characterized by a lack of appropriate social behavior.

Schizophrenia. Many children with autism were misdiagnosed with schizophrenia in previous decades. This mental illness, characterized by hallucinations and delusions, rarely arises before age seven.

Your Child's Unique Developmental Profile

A diagnosis gives a name to your child's developmental problems. But it's even more important to understand your child's unique developmental profile, the combination of strengths and vulnerabilities that make every child an individual. This point is especially emphasized by our advisory board member Dr. Stanley I. Greenspan in his book *The Child with Special Needs* and is the backbone of the intervention model he developed, DIR/Floortime. He stresses that children with the same diagnoses can have varying developmental profiles. For example, many children with autism learn best by seeing, but others learn better through sound or touch. Some are physically awkward; others move with grace and speed. Likewise, some children with speech disorders avoid social situations, while others are highly social despite their impaired speech. So, before you decide on any treatment for your child, always consider these areas:

Sensory Processing. How well does the child understand and use what she hears, sees, tastes, smells, and feels? Does she learn better by seeing than by hearing? Does she feel objects to learn about them?

Sensory Modulation. Is the child over- or underreacting to sounds, light, touch, movement, or other sensations? Is she constantly seeking or avoiding certain sensations?

Communication. How well does the child understand and use nonverbal communication, such as gestures and facial expressions? How much language does he understand or use? Is he able to articulate his words intelligibly? Is he engaging in sustained back-and-forth communication or only using language or gestures to make one-way demands? Do his words, sounds, or gestures have meaning?

Social. Does the child want to be with other children or adults? Is she able to indicate her interest in appropriate ways? In what situations does she approach people or avoid them? Does she seem attached to parents or other primary caregivers? Is she more engaged with some people than with others? Does she read and understand subtle social cues and rules?

Emotional. How well does the child regulate her emotions and moods? Is she generally happy and calm? Agitated and irritated? Anxious? Depressed? Does she swing rapidly from one emotion to another? What triggers her emotional changes? Does she understand the emotions of others?

Cognitive. How easy is it for the child to learn? Can he think and solve problems with logic and creativity? Does he think only in concrete terms, or is he able to use abstract ideas and engage in symbolic play? Can he understand and expand on the ideas of others?

Motor Skills and Planning. How well can the child use his hands? Does he have the mouth control needed to eat and speak? How does he use his larger muscles to walk, run, and climb? Does he have trouble planning and carrying out complex sequences of action, like putting on shoes or washing and drying his hands? Is he able to imitate the actions of others?

Attention. Does the child pay attention to the people and events around her? How hard it is it to get and keep her attention? Can she focus on activities she chooses herself? On activities initiated by others? Is she easily distracted by sights and sounds in the environment?

To Do Now

Learn your family history. As you work through the diagnostic process with your child, you'll find yourself answering dozens of questions about his health and developmental history. You also may face some questions about family history—and suddenly realize you don't really know much about it.

Was your eccentric uncle just shy, or did he have what today would be recognized as Asperger syndrome? Did your father suffer from depression, or was it bipolar disorder? Is it possible that your mentally disabled cousin had fragile X or some other genetic syndrome? Do you come from a long line of people with immunological disorders?

Such information could help you get a diagnosis and appropriate treatment for your child. It also might allow your child and family to participate in certain kinds of research, research that could someday help your family and many others.

Part Three

Helping Yourself, Helping Your Child

The initial waiting and worrying are over. Your child has been tested and retested, observed, analyzed, poked, prodded and, finally, diagnosed. You deserve to breathe a sigh of relief and to congratulate yourself for a job well done. Go ahead. Also take a moment to absorb what you've learned and to talk about it with family members and friends. Spend some time with your child, too, and remind yourself that he is still your child, not this new, scary label.

Now, take a deep breath, get your pen and phone again, reconnect to the Internet, and prepare, once more, to be overwhelmed. After all, a diagnosis only tells you what the problem is. It doesn't tell you what to do about it. It doesn't tell you how to treat your child or how to live, day to day, under the stress of managing his disability.

As always, your best source of information and inspiration is right before your eyes: most of the answers are there in your child. His unique developmental profile—the pattern of strengths and vulnerabilities you've come to recognize—will be your constant guidepost through the next, crucial steps.

In the next two chapters, you'll see how to cope, connect, and make smart choices as you travel from diagnosis to treatment—and to a better life for you and your child.

Chapter Seven

Time to Learn, Connect, and Cope

One mother remembers the day a doctor diagnosed her three-year-old son with PDD-NOS. After the appointment, her husband started reading aloud to her from a pamphlet the doctor had just handed them: "It basically said, 'Your life is over, just pack up your kid and put him in an institution,' " she recalls. "It said there are no real treatments. There are some options you can try, but these children are not going to talk, they're not going to do this and that. My husband read it and he had my son in diapers at the age of thirty. I didn't read past the first page. Instead, I went online and looked up PDD-NOS and got a better handle. I decided to listen to other parents and the people who work in this area. And I found out the picture was not so terrible."

Today, this woman's son is eight—and has been out of diapers for years. He's doing well in second grade, with a little help from a classroom aide. Though he struggles with conversation and social skills, his parents can easily imagine him going to college. They believe that appropriate therapies, paired with an unwavering faith in their child's potential, have made the difference.

But what will make the difference for your child? How can you possibly know what choices to make or whom to believe about your child's true potential?

When your child is newly diagnosed with a developmental

disorder, you may feel as if you've been given a new, impossible-to-fulfill job title: Parent in Charge of Separating Fact from Fiction, Knowing and Understanding Everything, and Making Perfect Choices. And you get this job assignment while caring for a child whose special needs may be exhausting you already. The stress can be crushing, the demands overwhelming.

> You're suffering all this pain and anxiety and your family
> is in turmoil. Then you have to decide how to somehow
> move forward and make a positive out of a negative.
>
> *Fred Wayne of Delaware, father of Derrick,*
> *diagnosed with childhood bipolar disorder,*
> *ADHD, and anxiety at age three*

More than one parent has taken a day to just pull the bedcovers over their heads and cry. If you need to do that, go ahead. Then get up and get busy. There's so much you can do, if you only reach out and connect with a world of information and support.

Reading, and Reading Between the Lines

Most people start their self-education by reading. Years ago, that might have meant going to the library to check out a few books and look up a few dusty medical journals. Maybe you'd also get some information from your child's doctor or teacher.

In those days, parents often had no access to the latest research on their child's disorder. Instead, they often were stuck with incomplete and outdated information. One mother, whose children are now teenagers, remembers going to a medical library to read up on their genetic disorder, and finding only grim, twenty-year-old accounts of institutionalized children who were given no chance of improvement. She and her husband left the library in tears. Months later, they connected with experts who could share a brighter, more up-to-date view.

With the Internet, that's all changed, mostly for the better, but also for the worse. Go right now to your favorite search engine and type in "autism." Now try it with "speech disorder," or "sensory integration dysfunction." You'll see the problem. Literally thousands of links pop up, some pointing you to highly regarded national support organizations and books by respected medical authorities; others to research findings from both known and unknown sources; still others to loosely organized parent chat and e-mail groups; and a good number to websites set up by individual parents or practitioners, many promoting particular treatments or products.

What should you read? And, more importantly, what should you believe? While most parents will be unable to resist the urge to dive into this vast array of material, it does pay to get a few solid facts under your belt first. Get an overview of your child's disorder. Once you know the basics, it will be easier to sort through everything else.

If possible, start by reading one or two straightforward, factual books on your child's disorder (see www.firstsigns.org for recommendations). Good books are available about all but the rarest conditions. Learn all the details that may have been omitted by the person or team who diagnosed your child. Find out what treatments are most widely used and why. As you read, constantly ask yourself about what might or might not apply to your child.

Next, read some research—not just whatever you stumble across online, but research that has undergone professional review. Remember, anyone, including people with products to sell and parent training programs to fill, can conduct a study. The most reliable studies are those that have been reviewed by other scientists and published in reputable medical and professional journals. One great place to find this kind of research is the database kept by the National Library of Medicine (see Resources).

As you read studies, ask yourself:

- Was this study conducted on children like mine? It's not enough to know whether the children in the study had the same diagnosis. You should also look for whether they were of the same age, had similar developmental profiles and similar health histories.

- If a study shows a treatment benefit, how strong was the effect? Did certain children benefit more than others? Did the study include any evidence that this treatment is better than others? Did the researchers rule out the possibility that improvements were due to other factors, including other treatments the children got at the same time?
- Does the study spell out any risks or side effects? How severe and how common are they?
- If a treatment showed no benefit, did the authors conclude that it was useless, or leave open the possibility that it might still work for some children?
- Are the results repeated in other studies, by other researchers? Have they been refuted? How many times?

A word of caution: much of the research available on developmental disorders, including autism spectrum disorders, has not yet passed the most rigorous kind of scientific testing. You will run into many studies that suggest a treatment is promising, but that fail to prove it is any better than any other treatment. You will run into many studies that fail to show a treatment works, but that also fail to show it does *not* work. The field is full of dedicated, honest researchers who simply have not had the resources to do the large comparative studies that answer those kinds of questions. There also are some bad eggs who take advantage of the research dearth to spread anecdotal reports—stories of apparent success in a handful of children—and to exaggerate the strength of their findings.

Keep in mind, though, that many of these understudied treatments, even some touted in thin, anecdotal reports, may turn out to have value. We just don't have enough science to know. In the meantime, parents and professionals simply have to consider which approaches are backed by the most evidence and which make the most sense for individual children.

I spent endless hours searching the Internet to try and find which interventions were "real" and which were "fake" and a waste of time. I slowly learned to check my sources and weigh the information I received. I had to become my own expert, for my son's sake.

Brenda Eaton of Pennsylvania, mother of Brendan,
diagnosed with autism at age three

Once you've read some research, go ahead and dive into that free-for-all on the Internet. Search around and read what professionals say. And read about the experiences of other parents and children. The Web is full of stories of hope and heartbreak, told by passionate, dedicated parents. Just remember that each story of an apparent miracle and each story of disappointment is just that: one parent's story, filtered through that person's beliefs and experiences and focused on one child, who may not share your child's underlying strengths and challenges. Likewise, once you've read a few books by professionals, go ahead and read some of the wonderful books written by parents of children with developmental challenges. (See www.firstsigns.org for recommendations.) You will find books that tell of remarkable, inspirational recoveries. And you'll find stories of parents coming to terms with profound, lifelong disability. Just remember: your child, like every child on earth, will write his own, never-to-be-repeated life story.

Knowledge is power. Everything I could get my hands on, I read . . . But you really need to focus on your child and be aware that not everything you read relates to them.

Penny Kelly of Connecticut, mother of Katie,
diagnosed with sensory integration
dysfunction at age two

Seeking Support, Parent to Parent

For many parents, reading about the experiences of other families is not enough. You have so many questions. And you are dealing with so many new feelings, feelings that your friends and relatives with typical children may not understand. So, eventually, most parents connect with other parents, both online and in person.

Online connections are easy to make. Many advocacy organizations maintain e-mail groups and chat rooms for parents. And there are many online groups started by parents themselves. With a little bit of searching, you can find a group for even the rarest disorder, and hundreds of groups dedicated to more common conditions. Often you can join the group and review message archives before you start to participate yourself. This will allow you to get the flavor of the ongoing dialogue. Before you join the discussion, ask yourself a few questions:

- Do these parents have children like mine?
- Does the group seemed focused on sharing information, sharing feelings, or both? Is the kind of help offered the kind I want?
- Is the group dominated by a few people or a few viewpoints?
- Do people treat each other with respect? Are there frequent arguments?

If you like what you see, go ahead and post a message introducing yourself and giving a little background about your child. See what kind of response you get, and go from there. Some parents use these online groups only to gather information and share practical tips. Others pour out their hearts to people they have never met. It's a very personal choice.

> When I was at the end of my rope, I posted a general cry for help and got great suggestions.
>
> *Karin Cather of Virginia, mother of two boys*
> *with autism spectrum disorders*

For most people, it's a good idea to at least try the old-fashioned alternative: the in-person support group. You often can find such groups through Early Intervention or school programs. Private agencies, therapists, and advocacy groups also host parent support groups. And sometimes parents form them on their own. There are even specialized groups for fathers and siblings. One dad who attended a group for fathers says, "It really helped to hear that it was not uncommon for other dads to break down and cry and grieve."

For a first experience, it's probably best to try a group organized by a professional, often a social worker or psychologist with a background in counseling parents in crisis. Before you attend a meeting, ask the leader about the goals and format. Is the focus on information or on feelings? Is the group only for parents with newly diagnosed children, or will it also include some veterans? Will there be guest speakers? If you still are interested, go to a meeting. You will quickly learn if the group suits you.

> When I first went to a support group, Michael had been diagnosed about a month. I went with my mother and we ended up supporting the other people. The leader was very nice but the people there were miserable and I wasn't, so I didn't go back.
>
> *Ida Palmieri of New Jersey, mother of Michael,*
> *diagnosed with autism at age two*

The first group I tried was a disappointment. I found myself, along with several other parents, trapped in a room with one mother who monopolized the conversation for an excruciating hour each week. Her main goal seemed to be talking herself, and us, out of believing that her son really had an autism spectrum disorder. I felt for her, but she wasn't doing anything to help the rest of us or herself. When other parents spoke up in this group it was mostly to talk about their sadness and anger—a real need for some people, but not what I wanted, at that point. Months later, I found a better group for me. It was organized by my daughter's school and was focused on sharing tips and resources. Often, we had a guest speaker on a particular topic, such as toilet training, medication, sleep problems, or behavioral challenges. Going to that meeting each month gave me a great lift. It was one more thing I was doing to help Sarah and help myself.

Navigating a support group can be tricky, even when the emphasis is on positive exchanges of advice and information. For example, when another parent gives you advice on a therapy to try or professional to see, you may appreciate it—or you may feel he's criticizing you for making other choices. When someone talks about the great progress her child has made, you may feel happy for her and inspired by her child's story—or resentful, if your own child isn't doing as well. (You may feel all those things.) You also may hear other parents talking with great conviction about beliefs you do not share, child-rearing practices you frown upon, or treatments you strongly believe are worthless. And it can be very difficult to discuss those kinds of differences without wounding feelings. That's why having a skillful moderator can be essential.

One mom told me about an enlightening experience she had in a group for parents of preschoolers with autism. At the first meeting, this mother bristled quietly as the invited speaker, the mother of an older child, read aloud a widely known essay that says having a disabled child is like planning a trip to Italy but ending up in Holland instead. The idea is that life turns out differently, but has just as many rewards. This mother had read the essay before—and felt angered by it. At the time, her five-year-old was still having toileting accidents that left her scraping feces out of his clothing several times a week; he also was having hour-long tantrums and biting her. She did not feel as if she were living in a nice, clean, scenic country. But she said nothing as the other mothers in the group nodded and smiled through the reading. Months later, at the group's final meeting, the social worker leading the sessions asked the mothers how they'd liked the various speakers. One mother said she had been really comforted by the reading of the Holland essay and that it had expressed exactly how she felt. Then the social worker asked the others what they thought: all six of them felt, as my friend did, that the essay was telling them it was wrong to feel that their lives were harder than those of other parents. While they hoped to reach Holland someday, they weren't there yet. Luckily, the social worker was able to lead the women through a discussion in which all of them—including the one who embraced the essay—felt heard and respected.

That's why so many parents show up at these meetings and spend hours drinking bad coffee and sitting on hard chairs: they want to be heard. They also want to listen, to other parents who know what it's like to have a child who doesn't speak or who throws violent tantrums or runs naked in the yard. They want to feel less alone, less isolated. And they want to know what to do. Often parents know more than any single professional. After all, your child's neurologist probably hasn't sat through an IEP meeting or had a chance to compare the three different speech therapy practices in town; your child's teacher has probably never been to the local children's hospital or set up a sensory integration room in her basement. But any one parent sitting next to you at a Tuesday night support group may have done all that and more.

Getting Individual Help

Sometimes, though, parents need more than information and casual support. Learning that your child has a disability and then living, day to day, with that disability is a major life stress. You may be emotionally drained, physically exhausted, and pushed to the breaking point by the sheer immensity of your daily responsibilities. Add the financial strain and marital stress that so many parents feel, and you have a recipe for total meltdown. The extreme pressure on parents in this situation is so well recognized that when one group of researchers wanted to measure the effect of stress on aging, they recruited mothers of children with autism and cerebral palsy as study subjects (and found that those who perceived the most stress were indeed aging faster than their peers).

I could not sleep at night, my stomach was in constant knots, our marriage was in a constant state of stress, and my entire world turned upside down. I questioned everything I ever believed in from both a spiritual and rational perspective.

Fred Wayne of Delaware, father of Derrick,
diagnosed with childhood bipolar disorder,
ADHD, and anxiety at age three

If you need extra, professional help to cope with your anger, sadness, anxiety, or guilt, get it. Set up an appointment with a psychiatrist, psychologist, or social worker experienced in helping parents in crisis. If you are so angry that you are lashing out at people or if you are so depressed that you can't function, get help immediately. Whatever you are feeling—whether it's grief over the loss of a "perfect" child, guilt over your perceived parental shortcomings, or anger at your child—you are not alone. Even if you have never heard another parent share those feelings, they are common. After all, any parent who has gritted her teeth while pulling a screaming toddler out of the toy store knows what it's like to be angry at a child. A parent raising a child who struggles to communicate, relate, and regulate emotion may find herself trying to control that kind of anger many times each day. In his book, *Special Children, Challenged Parents,* Robert Naseef, a psychologist who raised a son with severe autism, says he discovered the depth of his own anger late one night while cleaning up feces that his son had spread around his bedroom and body: "I was so furious at him for doing this to me—for making me go through this when most other five-year-olds, even with disabilities, knew better—I wanted to throw him out that window in his room; I really did. I didn't touch him, however, except to lead him to the bathtub and start cleaning him up."

Like Naseef, most parents control their anger. But anger needs to be expressed. So does sadness, especially when it deepens into depression. Private counseling sessions help many parents find a way to acknowledge and manage these strong feelings. Antidepressants and other medications also can help some parents get through a rough time. Some may put off getting this kind of help because they think it's wrong to focus time and money on themselves when their children need so much. But, remember, what your child needs most is you. Taking care of yourself will help you to take care of your child.

If support groups aren't for you, and you don't feel you need professional help—or if those outlets just aren't enough—try keeping a journal. Write about your feelings and daily struggles. Whatever you do, don't keep it all inside.

Getting a Break

Psychotherapy, medication, or professional counseling can be helpful. But sometimes, what a beleaguered mother needs is a bubble bath, a massage, or an hour with the Sunday newspaper. Sometimes, a worn-out father needs to watch a baseball game or drink a glass of wine before dinner. And all parents need to get out of the house. When you have a child with a disability, doing those simple things can often seem impossible. Your child may demand all of your attention when you are at home and may seem too demanding to leave with a babysitter or at a day care center. That's one reason why so many mothers and a few fathers of disabled children quit their jobs, even when they are desperate for money

Our entire life has been paralyzed by Noah's issues. He needs constant, one-on-one, moment-to-moment supervision if he's not in our home, and he can be so destructive that we don't go anywhere. He tries to escape everyplace we go—even out of moving cars. So we can't go to movie theaters, restaurants, playgrounds, or (without a lot of preparation and exhaustion) swimming pools. And I had to quit work, and my husband works seventy hours a week to make up my salary.

Karin Cather of Virginia, mother of two boys
with autism spectrum disorders

One mother of an extremely hyperactive, nonverbal three-year-old girl with a seizure disorder says she fears for her child's safety every time she leaves her with a relative or babysitter: "People don't understand that you have to watch her every second."

Every parent needs a break. So, no matter how hard it seems, try to find other people who can sometimes take care of your child. Offer them training, if need be, so that they know how to respond to his needs and keep him safe. If you have family members or friends who know your child well and are comfortable caring for him, you are very fortunate. Make use of these loving grandparents, aunts, cousins, and neighbors and let them know how grateful you are. If you don't have this kind of support, life is much harder. The high-school babysitters who watch all the other children on the street may not be up to the task of watching your child. Even professional nannies who pride themselves on managing all sorts of children may still have no idea what to do with a child who lacks basic play, communication, or social skills. (In a few communities, nanny services for children with special needs are arising, but they are extremely expensive.)

Some families with disabled children will qualify for publicly funded respite services that provide trained caregivers for a few hours a week. In some communities, religious organizations or other private groups give parents a break by providing disabled children a few hours of recreation and trained supervision on weekends. Some even offer occasional overnight care.

But, for most parents, getting a break means finding small moments of time—the five minutes during which your child is engaged in independent play, the forty-five minutes while he's in OT, the three hours while she's in preschool, the one night a month when you can get a babysitter—and making the most of them. Get creative with these pockets of time and be generous with yourself. While it's always tempting to use any down time to run another errand, check your e-mail from work, or clean the house, save some moments for yourself. It's good for you and good for your child.

If you have five minutes,
- close your eyes and do some breathing exercises
- have a cup of tea
- read the comics

If you have forty-five minutes,
- read a book that has nothing to do with your child's disability
- call a friend
- squeeze in a coffee date
- take a brisk walk
- take a nap
- listen to soothing music

If you have three hours,
- have lunch with a friend or your spouse
- prepare a special meal
- get a massage, haircut, or makeover
- take an exercise or yoga class

If you have a whole evening,
- have dinner and a movie with your spouse or a friend
- go to a book club meeting
- go bowling
- attend the symphony

I know how hard it can be to follow this kind of advice; I fail to follow it with great regularity. I exhaust myself trying to keep up with the professional work that I love while taking care of the daughter whom I love more than anything. My friends and colleagues get many a three A.M. e-mail from me and routinely scold me for going without rest. Rare moments away—even those five-minute cups of tea—are precious and necessary. Someday, I'm going to use all twelve of those coupons for free massages that one good friend gave me.

> Doing Tae Kwon Do helps. I get to yell and hit things and scream and it's socially appropriate!
>
> *Karin Cather of Virginia, mother of two boys*
> *with autism spectrum disorders*

Nurturing and Connecting with Your Child

No matter what your child's challenges, no matter what his diagnosis or prospects for the future, he is, most importantly, your child. The little girl lining up her blocks on your kitchen floor may not behave like the child of your dreams, but she still needs, just like any child, to be the love of your life. And you need it, too. While finding the best treatments and educational programs is important, finding a way to connect with your child, to nuture her and be her parent, is even more important. Sometimes, when a child has developmental problems—and especially when she has trouble connecting and communicating—parents may feel like they don't know how to parent. How do you express your love to a child who won't even look at you? How can you enjoy your time with a child who doesn't know how to play? The best answer is to follow your heart and your child. Your heart will tell you that this is the same child you fell in love with when he was a baby. And your child will tell you what he needs and enjoys, even if he never says a word.

So here's what to do with the little girl lining up the blocks: Get down on the floor and line up blocks with her. If she doesn't seem to notice, push a block out of place. If she looks at you, you've just made a connection. You've also mastered the first step of Floortime, the method that became the centerpiece of my own daughter's emotional, social, and intellectual growth. But forget about therapy for a minute. Just do whatever you can to share an experience with your child. Look out a window together. Run around in the snow. Share a bowl of popcorn or a walk through the woods. If he loves to sing, see if he will let you sing along. If she loves to hide under the bed, find out if there is room for two.

If your child is able to be close to you in any way, seek out and treasure those moments. From the time Sarah was an infant, I established our nighttime routine of snuggling in bed together. At first, I breast-fed her or gave her a bottle. Then, it became our reading time. Years later, we're still snuggling. Every night, I tell Sarah how much I love her and how proud I am of all her accomplishments. And she tells me that she loves me, too. No matter what, this is our sacred time together. We also spend many afternoons and weekends playing together and enjoying girl stuff. We give each other massages and facials, paint our fingers and toes, play Monopoly for hours, and go on imaginary vacations. Sometimes, we just giggle ourselves silly.

> In many ways, I feel that we are closer to our kids than other parents are. They are the focus of our lives and they get a lot more attention from us. I love my boys and know for sure that they love me, too.
>
> Joy Johnson of Maryland, *mother of two boys*
> *with autism*

Read the research, study up on the treatments and fight like a bulldog to get your child the services she needs. But first, and always, take care of yourself and your child. When you do, everything else will be much easier. And—whether you end up in Italy, Holland, or somewhere much more exotic—you and your child will have the best life possible.

To Do Now

Take a deep breath—literally.

If you've recently learned that your child has a developmental disorder, you are under life-changing stress. Experts say one of the best ways to tackle stress is to find a few moments a day just to relax and breathe deeply. You can do it in the car, in a waiting room, or even while waiting your turn to talk at a meeting.

The Harvard psychologist Alice Domar calls this technique a "mini-relaxation" and describes it in detail in her book *Self-Nurture: Learning to Care for Yourself as Effectively as You Care for Everyone Else.* Yoga and meditation instructors often teach their own versions.

In short, try the following:

- Sit up straight or lie flat on your back.
- Place your hand just below your navel, so you can feel the rise and fall of your belly.
- Inhale deeply through your nose and slowly count: "One, two, three, four."
- Pause.
- Exhale slowly, counting, "Four, three, two, one."
- Repeat several times.

~ Katie's Story

The baths are what Penny Kelly, a Connecticut mother, remembers most. Baby Katie hated them. In fact, Katie seemed to hate any sensation of cold or heat. And there was something about her mouth: as a toddler, she would stuff her cheeks with food, and she did not babble or speak. Mostly, she moved: climbing, spinning, hanging upside down, anything but sitting still.

At age two, Katie was diagnosed with sensory integration dysfunction. An evaluation team told Penny and her husband that children with this condition may recoil from too much noise, light, touch, movement, or even from strong tastes and smells. Or they may seem unfazed by sensations that would bother most young children—the wail of a siren, the pain of a skinned knee, or the sour taste of a pickle. Like Katie, they may seek out strong sensations—producing them by spinning in circles or stuffing their mouths with food—to compensate for their disordered senses.

For Katie, there were additional problems. She would weep when faced with the slightest change in routine, apparently because she feared an assault of unpredictable sensations. A visit to a busy store or a playground, even a pair of tight pants, could trigger a meltdown. And falling asleep during a car ride was the worst: waking up in a new place sent Katie into hysterics.

Penny especially remembers one Easter. Her parents had

invited the whole family to dinner at a restaurant. As a special treat, Katie rode with her grandparents. And the worst happened: she fell asleep during the ride and woke up in the backseat of an unfamiliar car, in the middle of a packed parking lot. "She was crying and screaming, and we could not get her out," Penny says. "She kept saying 'Lots of people, lots of people,' and we knew there was no way we could take her into that restaurant." Eventually, Penny and her husband coaxed Katie into their own car and started driving toward home. On the way, they stopped at a nearly deserted fast food restaurant. While the grown-ups ate their modest holiday meal, Katie climbed, ran, and crawled through the restaurant's play area. The more she moved, the more she relaxed. And, suddenly, it hit Penny: her daughter was happy and laughing, even playing with the only other child there. "It was a defining moment," Penny says, when she realized that, with the right support, her daughter could be as content as any child.

By then, Katie was already getting some help. The first elements were occupational and speech therapy, provided through Early Intervention. And Katie's therapists quickly discovered a key to progress: to benefit from a speech therapy session, Katie first needed an OT session focused on getting her senses in tune. So she would swing and climb, smear her hands with shaving cream, crunch her feet through a container of rice. Finally, she would blow bubbles and toot on whistles, warming up her undersensitive mouth before beginning to work on sounds and words.

At home, Penny looked for more ways to engage and coordinate her daughter's senses. Unlike other moms, she encouraged her daughter to jump on the beds and to tear apart the sofa cushions to make "Katie sandwiches." She put a big container of dried beans in the living room and hid little toys inside for Katie to find. And she encouraged messy play, with water and shaving cream, sand and mud.

Penny also learned to use homemade picture schedules to prepare her daughter for outings. If she wanted to take Katie to the grocery store and then the doctor's office, she would put a number 1 beside a picture of a grocery clerk and a number 2 beside a picture of the pediatrician. She also used pictures to help Katie make food and activity choices at home. And it all seemed to help: with a better understanding and more choices about everyday changes, Katie soon had fewer meltdowns.

At twenty-seven months, Katie said her first words: "Big Bird." On her third birthday, she said her first sentence. She had just emerged from a soaking on a water ride—an experience that might have unhinged her a few months before. Instead, she got off and said, "Oh, man, I need a towel!"

There were still some bumps along the way. When Katie moved to a special-needs preschool at age three, school personnel refused to combine her occupational and speech therapy sessions as her Early Intervention program had. And Penny had an unsettling meeting with a developmental pediatrician. Unlike any other professional who had seen Katie, this doctor believed that Katie was showing signs of an autism spectrum disorder.

Penny—who has a master's degree in education and has worked as a researcher and high school science teacher—had more confidence in her knowledge of her daughter. She rejected his suggestion outright. For one thing, she felt that Katie had good underlying social skills. She believed that her language delays, though pronounced, were rooted in her sensory difficulties and in other physical factors, including subtle structural abnormalities in her mouth and tongue, confirmed by later testing.

So, Penny says, "I just stuck with the therapies I knew were working for her." And, she added more. Among them was "hippotherapy"—a horse-riding program. At first, Penny would drive Katie an hour to the stables and watch as her daughter circled a horse for an hour, unable to touch the animal, much less ride it. After two months, Katie got on the horse. And she loved it. "She said her alphabet for the first time on a horse," Penny recalls.

Penny will never forget taking Katie for her first day of kindergarten, in a mainstream class. "She walked right up to the teacher and said, 'Hello, my name is Katie Kelly. Are you my teacher?' There were all these other children who were totally silent and my daughter was going around saying, 'Nice to meet you.' I wish that developmental pediatrician could have been there."

Today, Katie is seven and thriving. She does very well in school and has lots of friends. She enjoys herself at noisy birthday parties and recently cheered her way through a raucous professional hockey game. Motion remains her key to success: a schedule that includes gymnastics, dance, basketball, and tennis might be too much for some children, but is essential for Katie, Penny says.

"When I think about where she started and where she is today I am very, very proud."

Chapter Eight

Choosing Treatments

If your child was diagnosed with cancer, you'd fight for a cure. You'd dream, quite rightly, of her cancer-free future. But it's different when your child is diagnosed with autism or another developmental disorder. These are not "diseases" that can be rooted out of your child's brain with the right medicine or surgery. Whatever their causes, they are part of your child's neurological wiring. Certainly, some of that wiring can be rerouted. New, healthier connections can be made. And a few children who get early, intense help do grow up with no apparent disability. But have they been cured, or rather guided onto a healthier developmental pathway? Is there a difference? Parents and professionals struggle with these questions. Some are comfortable with the idea that some children recover completely. Others maintain that even the highest-functioning individuals retain some trace of their disorder, even if that trace is nothing more than a quirky personality or an unusual set of interests. Still others believe that stories of "cures" are cruelly misleading for the many parents who will do everything in their power to mitigate their child's disabilities and still face the lifetime task of supporting a son or daughter with special needs.

Someday, when we understand the brain and the causes of these disorders better, everyone may be able to talk about cures with confidence; we'll certainly be able to talk about prevention. But for now, it makes most sense to talk about caring for your child, not curing him.

> Our purpose was to help her, not to fix her. Our purpose was not to create a whole new child, it was to let her be herself—because she's a wonderful child.
>
> *Becky Wilson of Oregon, mother of Zoë,*
> *diagnosed at age four with developmental*
> *language disorder and "regulatory disorder*
> *with autistic behaviors"*

> I needed to do something to make him the best he could be, to grow up as happy and independent as possible.
>
> *Mary Barbera, mother of Lucas, diagnosed with*
> *autism at age three*

You can't know how far your child will go. But you can give him every opportunity to develop, learn, and enjoy life, just as you would for any child. The difference is that you will need to work much harder to open the doors that stand between your child and his potential. In fact, sometimes you will need a virtual battering ram. More than once, you may exhaust yourself opening a door only to find that you've merely entered another waiting room, or the wrong building altogether.

Keep pushing, and keep dreaming of the best possible life for your child. For some children, that will be a life in which their disorder, having been diagnosed early and treated aggressively, will someday play a minor role. For others, it will be a life in which the disorder, hard-wired and resistant to the best treatment efforts, poses profound, continuing challenges. But for all children, the fight for effective treatment is worthwhile, the potential rewards enormous. The only question is, Where do you start?

> There are no crystal balls here and there are no magic bullets, but there is a journey and that journey can

have many different trajectories. We want to optimize that trajectory.

Dr. Stanley Greenspan, child psychiatrist and
First Signs adviser

Where to Begin

As always, start by looking at your child. Even if that child has yet to say a word or use a meaningful gesture, she can point you toward her most urgent needs. Though every child is different, those most pressing concerns often fall into two broad categories:

- physical distress
- poor communication and social isolation

Physical Factors

Years ago, when I first started advising other parents, I would not immediately talk about the fact that many children with autism and other developmental diagnoses also had digestive disorders, allergies, sleep disturbances, and other health problems. I did not want to overwhelm parents by getting into a discussion of those issues at the same time they were struggling with the fact that their children did not speak or play. But over the years, I've been learning, along with many parents and many physicians who treat children with developmental disorders. Many of these physicians, including some at the nation's most respected medical centers, now believe that children with autism and other developmental disorders have, in years past, gotten inadequate treatment for all sorts of accompanying medical conditions. As a result, these children have suffered needlessly and learned and developed more slowly than they otherwise might. One doctor I know often tells the story of a ten-year-old girl with autism who was biting and hitting herself. Other experts said her behavior was just part of her autism and suggested antipsychotic medications. But this doctor, a gastroen-

Helping Yourself, Helping Your Child **161**

terologist, looked inside the girl's esophagus and found it was severely inflamed and covered with ulcers. The child, unable to describe the awful pain they caused her, had been lashing out at herself in anguish and frustration. A simple antireflux medication stopped the pain almost immediately, and with that the behavior disappeared.

If your child shows signs of physical distress (including diarrhea, constipation, vomiting, rashes, frequent ear or sinus infections, or unexplained aggression and tantrums), have them evaluated. After all, a child who is in pain isn't going to be very interested in learning how to play or speak, and he's not going to give his full attention to a therapist, teacher, or parents. So make his physical health a priority.

Doctors still aren't sure of the relationship between various health problems and autism spectrum disorders; they can't even say with certainty that children with autism and related conditions have more allergies and gastrointestinal difficulties than other children. One theory is that underlying immune system abnormalities contribute to both neurological and nonneurological symptoms in children with these complex, overlapping disorders. But, whatever the causes or links, it is clear that limited language skills prevent many children from effectively communicating their pain and distress.

Likewise, disturbed sensory function, so common in autism and related disorders, could play a role in creating or worsening some problems. For example, doctors commonly see children with constipation who get worse and worse because they fear their painful bowel movements; they also see children who soil their underwear because they don't sense the urge to defecate before it's too late to get to the bathroom. Also common are children with autism and other developmental disorders who have serious dental decay, often caused by a combination of poor eating habits and inadequate brushing—both, in turn, connected to a child's unusual sensory profile (which can lead to limited food choices and refusal to cooperate with grooming and hygiene routines). A child with a hurting mouth is almost always unhappy; a child who can't communicate that pain may be downright miserable.

In any case, every child with a developmental disorder deserves health care at least as attentive as that given to typically developing children. Don't let anyone tell you that your child appears miserable, has diarrhea, tantrums, staring spells, or odd movements "because" he has autism or some other developmental disorder. What if the diarrhea is caused by a food intolerance that could be relieved by a diet change? What if the tantrums are a response to easily treated pain? And what if the staring spells or odd movements are seizures, which eventually affect one third of people with autism and which can, in and of themselves, cause developmental delay and regression? (Such behaviors usually are not seizures, but you won't know for sure until you have them assessed by a neurologist or developmental pediatrician.) Your child deserves the kind of thorough medical care that would uncover these problems and provide effective treatment for them.

> What really tipped the scales for my son were the gastrointestinal issues. He was addicted to milk, tons and tons of milk. When we took him off milk and then put him on the gluten- and casein-free diet, he really improved a lot.
>
> Beth Corcoran of Massachusetts, mother of Joey, diagnosed with PDD-NOS at thirty months

Some doctors believe that treating immunological and gastrointestinal problems in children with autism spectrum disorders can directly improve brain function. Current biomedical and nutritional treatments don't cure autism, most of these doctors say, but may improve a child's ability to learn and connect with other people. Dr. Kenneth Bock, a New York physician who treats my daughter and who is a leader in Defeat Autism Now! (DAN!) a group of physicians dedicated to the health care of children with autism, puts it this way: "There's no question we need behavioral and educational therapies. But I think it's a mistake not to pursue the underlying biomedical problems . . . to do what we can to help the neurons function so they respond to all these therapies."

Some doctors and parents also believe that many children with autism and other developmental disorders suffer from toxic overload, particularly from mercury and other heavy metals. This theory is controversial and unproven, but some parents—including me—have found it convincing enough that we have tried treating our children with medicines that force their bodies to excrete metals. Studies on whether these treatments are safe and effective are under way.

An excellent book that provides much practical advice on using biomedical treatments for autism is *Unraveling the Mystery of Autism and Pervasive Developmental Disorder: A Mother's Story of Research and Recovery,* by Karyn Seroussi.

Communication and Connection

Beyond good physical health, the first thing most children need is a way to connect and communicate. Just imagine living in a world where it seems impossible to get what you want, whether it's food when you're hungry, a nap when you're sleepy, or a nice long walk when you're restless. It's no wonder so many children with communication disorders also have epic tantrums (even when they are not in physical pain). Many parents find that a child's behavior begins to improve as soon as they can communicate in some way, whether through pictures, words, or meaningful gestures. So finding a way to jump-start communication is often very high on a family's treatment wish list.

> Gabi used to just cry and I would never know what was wrong. When she learned how to point for what she wanted, it was a beautiful thing.
>
> *Debra Egan of New Jersey, mother of Gabi,*
> *diagnosed with autism at eighteen months*

Sometimes, though, a child is so disconnected from the world, so uninvolved in the people and activities around him, that he needs even more basic help: he must learn how to learn from other people. To make any other progress, these children must make the discovery that most of us make as infants—that other people are interesting and that interacting with them is worthwhile. Luckily, there are treatments that have helped many children make these leaps in communication and connection. In fact, there are lots of treatments. Your biggest challenge will be deciding which ones are the best for your child.

How to Choose

Someday, when we know more than we know today, it will be much easier to choose the right medicines, therapies, and educational approaches for children with autism and other developmental disorders. Genetic tests and other techniques will tell us the exact root of a particular child's problems. Reams of comparative studies will tell us which sorts of children respond best to which sorts of treatments, and which treatments don't work for anyone. In the meantime, parents must follow two guidelines:

- know your child
- know the treatments

By now, you should know a lot about your child: from the first moment you had a concern about him, through all the weeks or months of screening and testing, you've been putting together a more and more complete picture of his strengths and vulnerabilities. As you consider treatments, keep that picture of your child front and center. As you read or hear about any treatment or educational program, ask yourself key questions: Does this make sense for my child? Will it take advantage of his strengths? Help him overcome his greatest challenges? Keeping these things in mind will help you not only to choose particular treatments but to educate therapists, teachers, family members, and yourself about how best to apply any technique you choose.

For example, many children with autism and related disorders do not imitate others or respond spontaneously to children and adults. That's why many programs start with intense, individual, one-on-one therapy—therapy that coaxes the child into human interaction—rather than immediate placement in a traditional preschool or playgroup. The idea that the child is going to pick up better language and social skills from a noisy, busy classroom full of more typical peers, or children with various disabilities, is often a fantasy. However, every child is different. Some children with autism spectrum disorders and many with language disorders, attention deficits, emotional disturbances, mental retardation, or other problems do have the social awareness and imitative skills to benefit right away from well-chosen, well-supervised group activities.

And there are many other important distinctions among children with the same diagnoses. For example, one child may shrink from social interaction because he is extremely sensitive to sound and touch. Another may be just as aloof because he is undersensitive: he barely knows you're in the room with him. Those children may need different therapies and certainly will need to be approached differently by everyone who works with them.

Motor skills are another area of great variation. Some children lacking communication and social skills have great coordination and physical strength. Therapists and parents can take advantage of these children's highly developed skills to engage them in active, dynamic play. Other children have such impaired control of their muscles that they need intense occupational therapy to be able to benefit from the same kind of play. Instead of running obstacle courses and going on treasure hunts, these children might need to start by, literally, finding their own noses. And play for these children may need to focus on activities that do not require great dexterity—meaning that you put away the building blocks and get out the clay, forget about the tiny action figures and use huge stuffed animals instead.

Before you sign up your child for any therapy or educational program, go back and read any assessments you have, focusing on details about strengths and challenges. Look hard at your child. Think about what he needs most urgently and focus on that. Also keep in mind that all children need the ability to connect and communicate, to become part of the social world. That's always more important than learning any particular play or academic skill. A child who can build a castle of Legos and recite the alphabet but who can't share a laugh with you needs, more than anything, to be lured away from her blocks and letters and into meaningful interactions with people.

With those guidelines in mind, some treatment choices will be fairly obvious. A child with impaired speech needs speech therapy. A child with motor delays or sensory dysfunction needs occupational therapy. You may have questions about what kind of speech or occupational therapy is best, and you may need to do some research to find the best providers. Often you'll need to let your child attend a few sessions with someone to judge whether you are in the right place, with the right person. And you may have to fight your Early Intervention program, school system, or health insurer to pay for enough of these therapies.

Beyond that, things get complicated. There are dozens of therapies available for children with various developmental delays and disorders. Some are educational programs; others involve medications, vitamins, and diets; and others involve everything from horseback riding to music to eye exercises. How can you possibly know what's right for your child?

Start by doing some homework. Read those books and websites. Spend a few late nights perusing the research. And talk, talk, talk with the parents you meet at support group meetings and online. Find the most respected providers in your community and talk to them, too. If you are deciding between two or more major approaches, ask lots of detailed questions about how the programs would fit your child. Ask to see other children, in person or on videotape, receiving the therapy. And be on the lookout for informational workshops and seminars, hosted by local support organizations. (They're often a great way to meet a popular therapist or program director who might otherwise put you on a long waiting list.) If you are considering a classroom program for your child, visit the classroom and any alternatives. Talk with the parents who send their children to these programs. Interview the teachers and therapists. Find out about which methods they use, but also consider their personal qualities. Is this someone who will work hard for your child and treat you with honesty and respect? Armed with so much information and insight, you may be surprised by how easy it becomes to choose the best classrooms and therapies: eventually, you'll know them when you see them.

> In the first year, I didn't do the research and I depended too much on the professionals. I realize now that I can't do that. For one thing, autism is too complex.
>
> *Joy Johnson of Maryland, mother of two boys*
> *with autism*

Along the way, you will hear a lot of theories about which therapies and educational techniques are best. You'll hear providers and parents claiming that one or another major approach is the "only" one proven to work. You may even hear that mixing various approaches might somehow prove disastrous. Use your common sense. If you decide that your child needs highly structured behavioral therapy to learn basic skills, there's no reason you can't also try a little (or a lot) of free-flowing Floortime to expand his emotional and cognitive horizons. If you become a Floortime devotee (as I have), that does not mean you have to automatically rule out a classroom that uses a different approach to teach communication, academic, and self-help skills. (I ended up enrolling my daughter in a wonderful preschool classroom that relied on multiple methods, including some we did not use at home.)

Still, it may seem impossible to sort out all the approaches yourself. Rest assured, it's difficult for professionals, too. An expert panel, led by First Signs adviser Catherine Lord, spent three years reviewing autism treatment research. The panel's 2001 report, issued by the National Academy of Sciences, cited good evidence that a number of approaches can work but found no "clear, direct relationship between any particular intervention and children's progress." It said there was "virtually no data on the relative merit of one model over another." However, the report made some very important recommendations: it said that intervention for children with autism should be individualized and intense—consisting of at least twenty-five hours a week of year-round therapy—and should start as early as possible.

Give up the idea that you can (or must) make *perfect* choices for your child. Do your research, use your good sense, and get your child started on therapy. When something works, you will see results. When it doesn't, you can move on and try something else. And never forget: your child should lead the way. I remember one phone call with a parent who was trying out all sorts of treatments. As we were chatting, I heard a child in the background screaming as if someone were attacking him. So I asked the mother what was happening. She told me, "Oh, my husband is doing the brushing program on him and he hates it." She was talking about a widely used, often helpful technique in which the child's body is firmly brushed several times a day, in an effort to soothe and integrate his jangled senses. The mother told me they'd been trying the brushing for weeks. I gently suggested it was time to try something else.

Early intervention made a world of difference. And the fact that it was intensive and fit to meet his needs (and changed over time to meet his needs) made a difference. He always had a very tailored program. Definitely, without that, he wouldn't be where he is.

Brenda Eaton of Pennsylvania, mother of Brendan,
diagnosed with autism at age three

For one child, an individualized, tailored program might consist of a small classroom that includes some typically developing children, some speech therapy, supervised play dates, and a family-centered home therapy plan. For others, the mix will be much more varied and complicated—including all of the above, plus occupational, play, and behavioral therapy; medications; dietary restrictions; vitamins and supplements; auditory integration therapy; visual training; special communication techniques; and much more. Learn about your child and learn about the treatment options—and make the best choices you can.

> Once I became educated and talked to some supportive people (family and other parents of children with autism), I concentrated on doing what I thought was most beneficial to Michael. Also, I realized Michael would be fine if I was fine. So, I concentrated on all the happy moments and having fun, even if that meant we were spinning in the room for hours.
>
> *Ida Palmieri of New Jersey, mother of Michael,*
> *diagnosed with autism at age two*

Sarah's Treatment Story

My own daughter's treatment story is one of the more complicated ones. That's because her needs have been complicated. Between the ages of two and eight, Sarah was diagnosed with PDD-NOS, ADHD, colitis, multiple food allergies, bipolar disorder, and PANDAS—each one a complex disorder involving her brain, her immune system, or both. She was also, at age two, a child who showed a tantalizing potential for intellectual growth and emotional connection, but who was at great risk of never achieving that potential. I've had no choice but to fight for her future.

Like many children, Sarah started, at two, with a fairly basic program, arranged through Early Intervention. She got an hour of speech therapy and an hour of occupational therapy each week. It wasn't much, but even that little bit quickly showed results. Within two weeks, Sarah was using a few meaningful words. I was on fire with the desire to see her learn and develop more. So, within a short time, I also got her into a special twice-weekly play group. She also qualified for a home therapy program.

This home program introduced me to Floortime. Several times each week, energetic young women would walk through our front door and get down on the floor to persistently play their way toward connection with Sarah. Little by little, as I watched, these therapists started to reach her—winning a glance here and a smile there and, eventually, a bit of simple back-and-forth play. When they were gone, I would try to do the same. I would tickle her foot to get her to look at me and make a funny face to win a smile. When she would sit down with her shape sorter and start her routine—putting the blocks into the holes, over and over, in the same order—I would sit with her. I'd grab a block and laugh when she grabbed it back from me. Or I'd give her a mischievous look and put a block on my head. Sometimes I'd get a laugh in return, a glimpse at the delightful sense of humor growing inside my daughter. I was taking my first, untutored steps toward what would become a Floortime lifestyle.

Sarah started to blossom. I'll never forget the day I went to pick her up at her play group and learned that she had comforted another child. He had been sitting, sad and alone, inside a tent, and she had gone in and hugged him. It would have been a sweet, but small, moment for any typical two year-old; it was a huge leap forward for my daughter.

After a year of Early Intervention, Sarah was using more language and giving people her attention for short, precious moments. She would say "hi" or "bye," even to strangers. She was able to ask for help when she needed it, and her motor and cognitive skills were clearly improved. And yet, I wanted more. Much of Sarah's play was still solitary and repetitive. Much of her speech was repetitive and meaningless, too. She still spent a lot of time in her own world. I remember a day at the beach, watching Sarah run along the water's edge. I don't know if it was the roar of the ocean or the blinding sunlight, but she just could not seem to see or hear me. She seemed so isolated, so alone, running toward nothing and nobody. I wanted her to run to me—or, better yet, to run beside me, to share the sand, the sun, and the day with me.

I kept looking for more help. When she turned three, I enrolled her in (what I thought was) a promising new preschool program. But, in a classroom of six children with autism spectrum disorders, she was the only one with speech or rudimentary social skills. To make matters worse, the teachers used methods that were wrong for her. Within weeks, I knew she needed something else. While I searched for a better classroom, eventually succeeding, I also kept looking for other answers. Around this time, I attended a conference that changed our lives. In a darkened ballroom in the Virginia suburbs, I listened with excitement as professionals and parents talked in depth about the Floortime method. I liked what I heard. I already knew that Floortime had helped Sarah during her Early Intervention program and I continued to try my version during our hours at home together. I feared, though, that much of her potential remained untapped. So I made an appointment with Dr. Stanley I. Greenspan, the architect of Floortime.

A few months later, Sarah, my husband, and I visited the doctor's Maryland office. Dr. Greenspan turned on a video camera and told us to do our Floortime best. Well, that was tough. As the master watched, we each tried to engage Sarah. We followed her from room to room with a stuffed Barney doll, a telephone, whatever we could find, trying to get her to look at us, smile, say a word. We'd get a little something, here and there. Obviously, Dr. Greenspan said, she was relating to us, but she was also very self-absorbed, moving to her internal beat, not ours. And so, he started to coach us. Mostly, he used words like "more" and "bigger." He wanted us to use bigger gestures, more animated faces, more expressive voices. He wanted us to flirt with our daughter, to make ourselves so wonderfully engaging that she couldn't help but respond. And then we had to keep the responses coming, to close more and more "circles of communication"—his term for each back-and-forth volley of verbal or nonverbal communication. To succeed, he said, we would have to create a compelling, irresistible rhythm of interaction. The ultimate goal, he told us, wasn't more words or longer sentences. We were working instead for what he called "the gleam in the eye" and "the knowing look": a real sense of connection. We spent nearly three hours in his office that day and two hours the next with his colleague, Dr. Serena Wieder, a psychologist. She got down on the floor with Sarah and really showed us how it was done, eventually getting Sarah to engage in as many as fifteen back-and-forth exchanges of gestures, words, or expressions in a row. That was good, she said. But she and Dr. Greenspan wanted us to work toward doubling or tripling that capacity. This was not going to be easy!

We returned home with a therapy plan much more ambitious than anything we had tried previously. Dr. Greenspan prescribed six to eight sessions of Floortime, each lasting twenty to thirty minutes, every day. (Yes, that's two to four hours a day. But he explained that we could do it not only at home but also while buying groceries or even in the car.) He told us that most of this time could be unstructured and free-flowing, with no goal other than communicating and connecting at a higher and higher cognitive and emotional level. He also said we should use more structured games to teach Sarah specific language and thinking skills. In addition, he wanted us to target her sensory and motor planning difficulties by finding time every day to get her running, jumping, and spinning. He wanted us to stage treasure hunts and play catch, push her on swings and squeeze her between bean bags. But that wasn't all. He also wanted Sarah to have at least four play dates a week with a "verbal, interactive" child. He wanted us to change her diet. And, of course, he urged us to continue her speech and occupational therapy. He thought it would be all right if she continued to go to her special preschool—but, he said, just about everything else was more important.

It was an incredibly demanding list. How would we ever do all this? Or more accurately, how would I? By now, I had quit my job in corporate communications and was working full-time on only two things: helping Sarah and launching First Signs. My husband was busy with his own career and, increasingly, absent from home. Soon, with preexisting strains in our marriage stretched beyond repair, he would be gone altogether. Sarah's care was left almost entirely to me.

And yet, I believed that Dr. Greenspan was right: Sarah was already showing signs of communicative ability, warmth, and relatedness beyond what her initial diagnosis had suggested. With a great push, she might overcome many of her significant remaining challenges. So I pushed.

To the best of my ability, I did everything Dr. Greenspan suggested, and more. I turned the entire lower level of my house into a sensory and play area. We had a mini trampoline, a giant ball pit, and sand and rice bins stocked with hidden treasures; we had a quiet area with books and soothing music, a corner with musical instruments, an area with puppets and another area of tunnels and tents. Every day, we'd head downstairs and—with Sarah in the lead—create our own world of play and connection. We would spend hours chasing and hiding from each other. Sometimes she would run upstairs and hide on her bed beneath her pile of multicolored Teletubbies—Teletubbies were her central obsession between the ages of three and five—and I would find her. Or I'd pretend that I couldn't find her, and wait for her to pop out in glee. If she was interested in something, I was *fascinated* by it. Always, always, my goal was to keep the laughs and talk and smiles going, and to challenge her to move on to higher and higher levels of creative and logical thinking. If she was feeding her Teletubby Dipsy and suddenly walked away, I would try to lure her back in Dipsy's voice, asking "What happened? Why aren't you feeding me anymore?" The goal wasn't to get Dipsy another meal but to get Sarah to think and talk about about what she was doing. If Sarah said, "Dipsy, I'm all done. I want to rest," I'd try to get even more. I'd ask,

"Can we take a nap together?" The idea in Floortime is to keep up the purposeful dialogue, to close those "circles of communication," as Dr. Greenspan says. The more circles closed, the better; the more ideas generated, the better. Any back-and-forth communication is good; any back-and-forth communication that builds thinking and creativity is even better.

Floortime can be hard for some parents. It was for me, at first. After all, many adults don't know how to play with children. And, usually, no one teaches us. I'll admit that the bigger-than-life, all-out enthusiasm required did not come easily to me. But, once I knew what I was doing and why, I loved it. I didn't feel like a therapist; I felt like a mom.

Around this time, I also started taking Sarah to a wonderful play, speech, and language therapist, who worked with her first individually and later in a small group. Again, this was play with a purpose: "narrative play therapy," developed by our therapist, Ann Densmore. Dr. Densmore used Floortime methods to help Sarah tolerate and then welcome the presence of a playmate—and then to learn the fun of play itself, all while working on turn-taking, language and listening skills, emotional expression, and logical, creative thinking. One of Sarah's greatest challenges was learning to pretend. But by the time she was five, she was getting the idea: she finally appreciated that toy cars could go on imaginary shopping trips and exotic vacations and have horrible accidents and thrilling races; she learned that stuffed animals weren't just soft and colorful, but imaginary playmates who could share a cup of tea or try on new hats and coats.

Floortime and related therapies have always formed the centerpiece of Sarah's treatment. But her developmental and health problems, while no doubt connected by underlying biological factors, have been varied. So I have turned to many other treatments as well.

In the few months after she turned three, I realized that Sarah was having longer and more intense tantrums, despite her growing communication skills and social competence. She was volatile—quiet and self-absorbed one minute, overly talkative and manic the next. At any moment, she could completely melt down, screaming and crying, kicking and hitting. Months earlier, a doctor had suggested that I put Sarah on some kind of medication to help regulate her moods, but I had rejected the idea immediately. I did not see myself as the sort of parent who medicated a small child to improve her behavior. The whole idea rubbed me the wrong way. I thought there were always better alternatives.

Then came the driveway meltdown. After school one day, we went for a walk, as we often did. For reasons I'll never know, she lost it, just as we got into our driveway. She spent more than an hour in an intense rage, flailing her arms and kicking her legs, making it impossible for me to coax or carry her inside. She was by then a very strong girl and, though I tried over and over to get my arms around her and get her inside the house, I just could not do it without one of us getting hurt. And I could not talk her into coming inside under her own power. I was bruised, battered, and exhausted by the time she came through the door.

This was no way for us to live. I locked myself in my bedroom and, in tears, called the doctor who had suggested medication. We talked about the options, especially a drug called Risperdal. Originally used to treat psychosis, this medication has been shown in studies to regulate mood and behavior in children with autism spectrum disorders. I agreed to put Sarah on a small, trial dose.

The results were amazing. Within days, Sarah's horrible tantrums were gone and she was much less sensitive to touch. Suddenly, she wanted me to hold and touch her. This was a mother's dream come true. And her teachers noticed that she was more sociable and focused at school.

I'd like to say that was the end of our medication story, but it wasn't. Over the years, Sarah has made tremendous progress in her social, intellectual, and emotional life. But she continues to struggle with rages, which are sometimes controlled for a while, but always come back. In the beginning, the calm might last a year; then the storms would come again and I'd adjust Sarah's medication. Over the years, the good periods have grown shorter and shorter. Today, I feel blessed if the rages abate for a few good weeks. Sarah also remains wildly overactive, inattentive, and obsessive at times. All of these problems may be part of PANDAS, a diagnosis that has sent us in new treatment directions.

We have tried other medications—lots of them. My best guess is that there have been more than thirty and maybe as many as fifty, if you count every prescription drug she's ever ingested. We've tried the mood-regulating drugs (such as Lithium and Depakote) and the attention drugs (such as Ritalin and Strattera). A few have helped a little for a brief time, others not at all. Many have had unpleasant or scary side effects, and a couple have been downright toxic. I remember the night when, after a few doses of Strattera, Sarah projectile-vomited all over the bathroom floor, walls, and air vents and then slipped in the mess and nearly broke her tooth. I came to her aid, and fell into the pool of vomit myself. We ended up sitting there together, crying and laughing hysterically. What else could we do?

Today, Sarah is still on a low dose of Risperdal. It seems to work better than anything else, though not well enough. So we keep looking. In the past year, since the PANDAS diagnosis, Sarah has been taking daily penicillin (so far the only accepted treatment for PANDAS). We hoped it would keep the strep bacteria from attacking her immune system and her brain anymore. We think the bacteria are harbored somewhere in her body (we don't know where) and may be causing many of her problems. The antibiotic has eliminated most of the rages and minimized the obsessive behaviors, but it is harming her liver and her digestive system. Her poor little body can't take much more of it. So I am now looking into experimental treatments that might more directly repair her immune system and eliminate the strep.

Meanwhile, we continue another course of therapy we began when she was three: a complex regimen of vitamins, nutritional supplements, antifungals, and digestive enzymes. Sarah swallows about fifty pills a day and—though a few doctors have scoffed at this—I believe that they help to keep her mind and body as healthy as possible despite her underlying problems. Some of the substances she takes are thought to help with mood, but most are thought to benefit the immune system and gut. I am quite aware that little research backs this kind of supplementation, but anecdotal reports from parents and health care providers strongly suggest benefits for some children. In Sarah's case, I've been careful to add treatments like these one at time, watching for side effects and benefits.

I also limited Sarah's diet for several years. This is a practice based on the belief—also not yet supported by research—that certain foods contribute to the immunological and gastrointestinal difficulties seen in many children and may contribute, directly or indirectly, to their neurological problems. The diets don't seem to help all children, but anecdotal reports of dramatic changes in some have gotten the attention of many parents and practitioners. In Sarah's case, she had clear allergies to some foods (soy, wheat, barley, oats, rye, dairy, yeast, and a few others) and I wanted to try anything that might help her. Dr. Greenspan also strongly supported a dietary plan that eliminated foods that were possible troublemakers and added more fruits, vegetables, and protein. So, from the time Sarah was three until she was about six, she ate no gluten (found in wheat and other grains), dairy, soy, additives, or dyes. I did a lot of home cooking and careful shopping. It was work, but I'm convinced it was worthwhile. I saw her health improve as soon as I took away milk. I saw even more improvement in her health and behavior when I took away gluten, removing it slowly over a matter of months as I found substitutes that Sarah liked. Sarah's dad was convinced this was all a waste until she was five and—in preparation for a medical test—I gave her high levels of gluten for three days. She went into behavioral meltdown and suffered severe diarrhea. He asked me to never give her gluten again!

However, by the time Sarah got to first grade, she started to crave the cafeteria lunches and other things that her friends were eating.

Slowly, as it became apparent that her gut was healing and her allergies disappearing—thanks, I believe, to the diet, supplements, and other treatments—we added back most foods (except those with dyes and preservatives). I do think the restricted diet helped Sarah get through some crucial years. (The First Signs adviser Kelly Dorfman, a Maryland nutritionist, says that in her practice, about a third of children with autism spectrum disorders have a dramatically positive response to a gluten-free and dairy-free diet; another third see modest results; a remaining third don't benefit.)

And there's more. Once a month, I still drive Sarah, four hours each way, to get an intravenous dose of glutathione. This is a natural amino acid needed by the body to balance red and white blood cells, boost the immune system, and rid the body of toxic metals. Like many children on the autism spectrum, Sarah showed low levels of glutathione in blood tests. I am convinced that this experimental treatment helped to heal Sarah's gut, allowing her to eat regular foods once again.

Among the other treatments I've tried for Sarah:

- Chelation. After hair tests suggested Sarah was not excreting toxic metals like mercury, lead, copper, and tin, we tried two oral medications that can force the body to excrete the metals. Tests showed they did just that. And I thought Sarah did some particularly complex thinking and drawing during these treatments. She suffered no serious side effects (the treatments can cause behavioral disturbance and liver damage). We also tried some chelating skin creams, but those were ineffective—and too stinky for a child who needs to go out to school or camp every day.
- Auditory integration. We tried a listening therapy called the Tomatis Method when Sarah was four. It had a wonderful effect on her auditory processing. She seemed able to hear sounds that she had never heard before. However, it became difficult for us to maintain over a prolonged

period because of the expense. This is something I want to try again.

- Hippotherapy (horseback-riding therapy). Sarah loved this activity, which was supervised by an occupational thera-pist and intended to build her confidence and help with sensory and motor issues. But it was expensive and our health insurance stopped covering it. Given the expense, some other treatments were a much higher priority for us.

While this may sound like an impossibly complex treatment plan, I have made each choice with Sarah's most urgent needs in mind, and with the belief that while Sarah's various difficulties may have one or two underlying biological triggers, they still must often be addressed one at a time.

What would Sarah be like today if we had not done all these things? I'll never know for sure. But I do know that two years after our initial meeting with Dr. Greenspan—and three years after Sarah had been diagnosed with PDD-NOS—this is what the doctor wrote: "Sarah's engagement is wonderful. She's warm, engaged, sweet, and has a very positive affect. She's got the gleam in her eye and a zest for living. . . . She's able to participate in a continuous flow and reciprocity of back-and-forth conversation now. That's what separates a child without PDD from a child who has that disorder."

By then, Sarah's treatment had cost our family well over $100,000, much of it for experimental biomedical therapies that insurance companies don't cover. I'd gone literally years without enough sleep or leisure, had given up my well-paid career and my suburban dream house. I'd spent every available moment finding, paying for, or providing my daughter's therapy.

And every bit of it was worthwhile.

I am repaid every time I see my daughter laugh at a joke or sym-pathize with a playmate who's been rejected by another child. I am repaid many times over every time that she hugs me and says, "I love you, Mom."

Charting Your Own Course

What is the recipe for treating your child? Unfortunately, there is no cookbook, both because there is no standard child and because research on effective treatment is so lacking. The things I've done for Sarah have made sense to me and been right for her. Likewise, the other parents featured in this book, and the parents you will encounter in support groups, in waiting rooms, and online, have made choices that worked for them and their children. You will have to find what is right for your child.

How will you know whether you are on the right track and getting the best possible results? A few guidelines:

- Whenever possible, add one new intervention at a time, so that you can make some judgment about what's working or causing new problems. A child who suddenly starts having tantrums a week after starting a new medication, taking a new supplement, *and* joining a new classroom could be reacting to any or all of the changes. Likewise, a child who starts using words the month you change his diet and enroll him in speech therapy could be benefiting from either treatment, or both.
- Understand and respect the placebo effect. Children undergoing intensive interventions for autism and other developmental disorders often make significant progress—progress that may be independent of any particular treatment but that can easily be mistaken for a treatment effect, especially when parents, therapists, doctors, and teachers are eagerly watching a child for responses to a new therapy or medication. (In one study of the hormone treatment Secretin, doctors and parents reported a significant improvement in autism symptoms—but then found the improvements were just as likely in the children getting placebos as in children getting the real thing.)
- Keep data. This can be as simple as a daily written log

that describes how your child is feeling and acting. Note any changes in skills, behavior, moods, concentration, energy, sleep patterns, bowel movements, eye contact, social interactions, appetite, or physical symptoms (for example, rashes, eye circles, itchiness, hives, nausea, headaches). Some treatments may require you to keep even more detailed data about your child's skills and behaviors.

- Stay focused on what's most important. If a child is learning some academic skills but is not improving in her ability to connect with other people, regulate her moods and behavior, and learn from her environment, she may not be getting the therapy she needs most. If you see progress in these key areas, that's a great sign.

- Keep talking to the members of your team—teachers, therapists, doctors. Constantly ask for their impressions and share yours. If you have a new area of concern, discuss it. Let everyone on the team know what the others are doing. And, if at all possible, get them to communicate with one another.

- Make sure you know what's going on when your child is behind closed doors in a therapy session or classroom. You should have ample opportunities to observe your child. If you can't be in the room, because your presence distracts or disturbs your child, ask for a videotape of a session. If possible, volunteer in your child's classroom and never pass up an opportunity to visit for a party or field trip. And make an ally of the school nurse: ask her to help you monitor your child's health and alert you to any changes.

- Once you've chosen a treatment, do your best to apply it consistently. You won't be able to tell whether a diet change works if you allow a child a forbidden food every three days. You won't be able to tell whether a medication works if you skip doses.

- Don't let your school system or Early Intervention program get away with abandoning your child for the summer: most children with developmental disorders need year-round therapy to keep making progress.
- Make sure you do your part at home. If a speech therapist suggests some games, play them; if an occupational therapist shows you some techniques, try them. You will spend much more time with your child than any therapist, so make the most of it.
- As always, follow your child's lead and your own best instincts. If you are convinced something is helping, keep doing it. If you believe you are wasting time and money or, worse, harming your child with any intervention, stop it.

Along the way, you may encounter naysaying and resistance—especially if you choose treatments that are considered "alternative" by many in the medical and educational mainstream. Certainly, you should respect the expertise of your child's doctors, teachers, and therapists. It's especially important to consult your child's doctors when weighing the potential risks and benefits of any biomedical treatment, including diets, supplements, and medication. But always expect professionals to respect you as well. If you find yourself under attack for doing what you believe is right for your child, go elsewhere. Find doctors who are comfortable with today's real world, a world in which traditional and alternative approaches coexist. What's "alternative" today could be mainstream tomorrow.

Finally, remember: your most important job title isn't "therapist" or "case manager." It's "parent." Play that role with relish. Provide your child with appropriate treatment, but also with love and attention. And when your child makes progress, no matter how big or small, you will know that you have made a difference.

Treatments Available

The cornerstone of initial treatment for many children with autism spectrum disorders, and sometimes for children with other delays and disorders, are therapies that rely on intense one-on-one interaction and/or a specially structured teaching environment. The most popular of these approaches fall into three categories: developmental, behavioral, and organizational.

Developmental Approaches

These focus on filling in a child's basic developmental gaps, rather than teaching specific language, academic, social, or other skills. Often these approaches start by connecting with the child emotionally and using that connection to engage him in ways that will move him up the developmental ladder. These approaches include:

DIR/Floortime. In this "developmental, individual-difference, relationship-based" approach, parents are trained to act as the primary therapists, literally getting down on the floor with their children, often for twenty- to thirty-minute periods, several times a day. By meeting the child at his developmental level and by following his lead, the parent attempts to engage him in increasingly longer and richer streams of back-and-forth communication and meaningful play. The therapy focuses on using the parent-child relationship as a building block for broader learning and emotional growth. The techniques also can be used by schools and by play, speech, and occupational therapists.

Relationship Development Intervention (RDI). Parents also are the primary therapists in this approach, which starts by using a series of highly structured games and exercises to teach the child how to tune in to the actions and emotions of other people. The parent and child then move on to exercises that focus on back-and-forth communication, shared experiences and play, and, gradually, to less structured interactions that build social awareness and competence. Parents attend training sessions and also are supervised by therapists trained in the method.

Son-Rise. This method, taught by parents who helped a child overcome autism in the 1970s, emphasizes accepting the child and interacting with him in an enthusiastic, positive way, for many hours a day, in a specially designed home playroom. Parents and other therapists, who must attend training sessions, are encouraged to "join" the child in activites, like hand-flapping and repetitive play, that may be part of his disorder, but also to attempt to engage the child in more meaningful play and communication. No studies of this method have ever been published.

Behavioral Approaches

Based on a science called applied behavioral analysis (ABA), these methods focus on teaching the child specific skills and behaviors in a systematic, highly structured way, using constant rewards and repetition. The idea is to reinforce positive behavior (including all kinds of learning and appropriate social interaction) while reducing or eliminating behavior that gets in the way of learning and communicating. ABA programs often start with twenty-five to forty hours a week of therapy and can be conducted at home, at school, or both. As a child progresses, the program may become less structured and include more teaching during routine, daily activities. Parents may be trained as therapists, but most home therapy is conducted by college students, supervised by more experienced behavioral specialists. Particular types of ABA include:

Discrete Trial Training (DTT). This is the original and most structured form of ABA. A typical program for a child with classic autism might start by teaching the child how to sit in a chair and make eye contact and then proceed to teach language, academic, and social skills. Each skill is broken into small parts and taught in repetitive drills; therapists keep extensive data to track progress. The child is rewarded, often with bits of food, toys, or praise, for every appropriate response. Inappropriate responses are ignored or corrected.

Verbal Behavior (VB). This variation of ABA focuses on teaching language by breaking it into small, functional parts that can be taught in a systematic way. A program starts by assessing the child's existing communication skills in minute detail. Then a curriculum is devised to fill in the gaps. A typical program for a child with classic autism might start by rewarding him for responding to his name or for imitating a sound, and then teach the child how to make requests, label objects, ask questions, follow increasingly complex directions, and, eventually, engage in conversation.

Organizational Approaches

These focus on creating a physical environment and routine that maximizes a person's ability to function and learn. The most common method:

Treatment and Education of Autistic and Related Communication-Handicapped Children (TEACCH). This is primarily a classroom approach. It focuses on teaching children independent work and life skills, along with communication and social skills, and relies heavily on structured settings, predictable routines, and picture schedules—elements designed to build on the strengths and preferences of many children with autism spectrum disorders. Some parents also use elements of TEACCH at home.

In addition to these cornerstone approaches, most children with developmental delays and disorders receive a number of other therapies and treatments that fall into several categories:

Clinical Therapies

These are directly provided by specially trained professionals.

Speech and Language Therapy. Therapists help children improve their ability to produce speech and use language. Some also help children improve eating skills. And some teach alternative forms of communication for children who cannot speak. Therapy can occur at school, at home, or in private offices, individually or in groups. The techniques used vary widely, depending on a child's diagnosis and developmental profile. A typical session might include mouth exercises and carefully targeted speaking and listening games.

Occupational Therapy. Children improve fine motor, self-help, and eating skills and may also work on sensory integration during group or individual sessions at home, at school, or in private offices. Techniques vary depending on the child's needs. During a typical session, a child might use swings, crawl through tunnels, and play with shaving cream, sand, clay, and other materials. She might also draw pictures, construct puzzles, and use scissors, zippers, buttons, eating utensils, and other common objects. School-age children may also work on handwriting.

Physical Therapy. The focus is on large motor skills, such as crawling or walking, jumping, running, and using playground equipment. Goals often include increased strength, balance, coordination, and mobility as well as better sensory integration. Services can be offered individually or in groups, at home, at school, or in private offices. Techniques vary depending on the child's needs, but a typical session might include physical exercises and games, as well as practice using stairs, play equipment, or other items in the child's everyday environment.

Auditory Integration Therapy. Children listen to a special selection of modified music or other sounds in an attempt to correct problems with processing and understanding speech and other sounds. Listening sessions are clustered together over a few days or weeks. This is a widely used but still experimental treatment.

Vision Therapy. Exercises and sometimes special lenses are designed to retrain the visual system—the eyes and key brain areas—in children who have trouble seeing or trouble understanding and learning from what they see. This method, also known as eye training, behavioral optometry, or orthoptic therapy, is sometimes described as "physical therapy for the eyes."

Biomedical Treatments

Medications. Prescription drugs can be used to treat some symptoms, including hyperactivity, anxiety, tics, and mood instability, as well as accompanying disorders, such as seizures, allergies, and gastrointestinal problems. Many of the medications can have serious side effects, so their risks must be weighed carefully against potential benefits. Doses should also be kept as low as possible. Often, many different drugs are available to treat the same symptoms or conditions, so the best choices must be found through trial and error.

Chelation. Compounds taken by mouth, IV, or rubbed on the skin can be used to reduce toxic levels of heavy metals, such as lead and mercury, in the child's body. Some of the compounds carry a risk of liver damage and can cause or worsen gastrointestinal and behavioral problems. The creams generally have a foul odor as well. This is an experimental treatment for children with autism spectrum disorders, based on the theory that an overload of heavy metals, especially mercury, contributes to physical and behavioral symptoms.

Diet. Special food plans, including some that eliminate certain food groups, can be used to treat metabolic conditions, prevent allergic reactions, relieve gastrointestinal symptoms, or optimize nutrition. Dietary changes may also improve learning and behavior in some children, though this has yet to be proven in carefully controlled studies.

Vitamins and Supplements. Some doctors and nutritionists advise larger-than-usual amounts of certain vitamins and other nutrients for children with particular developmental and health profiles. The effectiveness of these substances is generally unproven, except in some rare disorders. Children should not take high-dose vitamins and supplements except under medical supervision.

Immunological Treatments. Therapies that can alter the immune system, including steroids and infusions of intravenous immunoglobulin (IVIG), are used to treat confirmed or suspected immunological deficits in some children. These treatments, which carry long-term health risks, are sometimes used in language-impaired children with certain kinds of seizures. Their use in other conditions is under study.

Secretin. This hormone has been reported to help some individual children with autism, but clinical studies, comparing secretin to placebos, have failed to show a benefit.

Additional Therapies

Augmentative Communication. Alternative forms of communication, which can include picture cards (such as picture exchange communication [PEC]), sign language (including American Sign Language), letter boards, and computerized devices, are used as primary, long-term communication strategies or as bridges to oral language.

Rapid-Prompting Method. In this technique, developed by the mother of a nonverbal young man with severe autism, a teacher uses rapid speech and other intense stimuli to keep the attention of a student and to prompt rapid responses from him. The idea is to teach students to respond by pointing to choices on a letter board or piece of paper. This technique has undergone no scientific study.

Facilitated Communication. In this controversial technique, a nonverbal person types on a computer keyboard while someone else supports his hand or arm. Several studies strongly suggest that in many cases, the thoughts communicated are those of the facilitator, not the disabled person. However, some individuals who start typing with a facilitator later type—and apparently communicate—on their own.

Music Therapy. A music therapist, working with children individually or in groups, can use singing, movement, and instrument play to work on language, communication, social, motor, and sensory issues.

Animal Therapy. Children, often guided by occupational therapists, interact with animals (often horses or dolphins) to work on sensory and motor issues and to build confidence. Some children also work with dogs and other pets to build relationship skills.

Play Therapy. A professional—often a social worker, a psychologist, or a speech therapist—engages the child in play to work on emotional issues, communication, and social skills. Therapists work with children individually or in groups and may employ techniques also used in Floortime, psychotherapy, or speech and language therapy.

Recreational Therapy. Participation in swimming, gymnastics, dance, art, and other activities (sometimes adapted for children with special needs) is recommended for some children. Many communities also offer summer camps for children with special needs.

Social Stories. Simple stories, composed with pictures and, sometimes words, are used to teach children social and self-help skills and to prepare them for changes in routine and new situations, from vacations to shopping trips. Parents and teachers can buy books containing basic social stories, but usually learn to write their own to meet the child's individual needs.

Social Skills Groups. Children get together to work on social and play skills, in groups overseen by a psychologist, social worker, or other professional participants. They learn the rules of social interaction and are trained to recognize and read social cues, show appropriate interest in others, and recognize and correct their own socially inappropriate behaviors.

To Do Now

Find out if your child might qualify for a treatment study.

Treatment for autism and related disorders can be extremely expensive. And when treatments are experimental—as many for these disorders are—insurers often won't pay for them.

So one way to get your child cutting-edge treatment, and to help find answers for other children and families at the same time, is to enroll him in a treatment study. Thanks to increased government funding and an increased public demand for answers, more studies are starting all the time.

To find out what might be available for your child:

- Go to www.firstsigns.org and click on "Research."
- Go to www.cureautismnow.org.
- Check with your closest university or research hospital.
- Ask your child's doctors and therapists.

~ *John's Story*

As an eighteen-month-old, John Scott could recite whole story-books after hearing them read aloud just once. And he never forgot a route. If his mother, Beth, went a new way to the grocery store, John would cry and scream, "Wrong way, wrong way," from the backseat. Beth, an editor, and her husband, Frank, an economist, were impressed with their son's memory. They also noticed that John had a "singsong" way of speaking and liked to repeat favorite words and phrases. But they weren't worried about those things. And neither was their pediatrician. The doctor did not raise "any red flags or yellow flags" at John's checkups, Frank recalls.

Still, Beth started to feel uneasy when John began preschool at two and a half. "He clearly liked being around other kids, but his way of approaching them was never quite right. If they were building something, he would go over and knock it down. Or he'd be playing in the sand and would dump sand on himself and on other kids. That was his way of saying he wanted to play. . . . And when they didn't want to play that way, he was devastated."

John was constantly breaking down in tears and frustration. But the staff at his preschool told Beth not to worry. A lot of the children—especially the boys—were still learning the basic social ropes. It was a "wacky age," they said. Other mothers assured

Beth that their children did exactly the same things. As the months passed, though, Beth got more worried. The other boys at school seemed to be maturing. John did not.

Finally, after a year, the preschool staff referred the family to a child behavioral therapist. The therapist immediately noticed that John had trouble with eye contact and conversation. Within a couple of visits, he mentioned "PDD"—pervasive developmental disorder. Beth did some online research. Her heart sank when she learned that PDD probably meant a kind of autism. "I went back to his office and asked, 'What are the chances that this is high-functioning autism or Asperger syndrome?' He looked at me and said, 'You've been doing your homework.' "

Beth and Frank took John to a clinical social worker who specialized in treating children with social skills problems. She confirmed that John fit the Asperger profile. He was clearly bright and had more than adequate language skills. But he did not know how to make a friend or have a simple, pleasant talk. Instead, he spoke in monologues about the things that interested him, like maps and dinosaurs. He constantly corrected and criticized other children, not seeming to understand that he was hurting their feelings. John started attending a social skills group and individual therapy.

Meanwhile, his parents had him evaluated by the local school system. The school team agreed that John was a strong learner but needed a lot of help to get ready for kindergarten. Not only were his social and communication skills lacking, but his fine motor skills were, too. So his parents agreed to enroll him for a year of special-needs preschool and occupational therapy.

By the next fall, John was getting along better with other children and seemed more easygoing. Everyone agreed it was time for him to return to a mainstream classroom. At first, he seemed okay. But within a couple of months, John began to argue and tussle with his kindergarten classmates. He had meltdowns when his schoolwork was difficult, and he refused to ask anyone for help. By the middle of the year, he was spending most of his day in a small special education group where he could get individual help and work on his social skills.

Over the past couple of years, with a lot of support, John has worked his way back into the mainstream classroom. Now aged nine and in third grade, he spends his whole day with his typical classmates, sometimes assisted by an aide or special education teacher. He struggles a bit with writing. He excels at math and science. His parents fully expect he'll go to college one day.

But, these days, college is the least of their worries. Instead, they worry most about John's continuing difficulties with other children. "He is very negative toward the other kids," Beth says. "When he sees someone acting silly, he'll snap, 'Oh, that's really stupid.' He'll say things that maybe other people are thinking, but don't want to say out loud." Though John can hold good conversations with adults—or, at least, with adults who know how to talk to him, in a quiet, calm way—he has a lot more trouble with children.

"For now, I can be his buddy," Frank says. He and John take hikes together most weekends, go to museums, and shoot baskets. "But I would like him to have another best buddy when he's thirteen years old."

John is increasingly aware of his social isolation. He's started to complain that he isn't invited to nearly as many play dates or birthday parties as his seven-year-old brother, Adam. Adam went to his first sleepover recently; John hasn't been to one yet. And, sometimes, John seems to take out his frustrations on his brother, calling him names and belittling him. Recently, the Scotts started taking Adam to therapy sessions, too. "Adam used to be 'Mr. Smiley,' but not lately," Beth says. "We worry that he's feeling beaten down and victimized by John."

Still, Beth and Frank remain optimistic for both of their boys. They hope that Adam will see that he can be a good role model for his brother and help him to get along with the world. And they hope John will find a niche as he grows. Maybe in middle school, he'll play an instrument and get to know other kids interested in music—or in math or science, they muse. Maybe some-day, he'll be a lot like his grandfather, a brilliant man treasured by his family but more interested in scientific trivia than in people.

"I think because we caught his problems so early and we're really still working so hard with him that he will make a lot more progress," Beth says. "I see him excelling professionally in what-ever field he chooses and having friends and colleagues within that world. I don't know. We'll have to wait and see. But I think he's always going to be a little bit odd."

Part Four
Second Steps and Beyond

You are the parent of a child with special needs. That means your life has changed. No matter how much progress your child makes, you and your family will never be quite the same. For one thing, you'll never again take any child's healthy development for granted. Now you know: all children need love and attention, but some children need even more from their parents, families, and communities. If you are at the beginning of this journey, you may wonder how you will ever keep up the pace over the many years ahead.

Rest assured that for most families, life gets easier. Children grow and change. Families adapt. Those who do the best do a few things especially well. They learn to accept their children, disabilities and all, even while fighting for every inch of progress. When they see their children move forward, whether by inches, feet, or miles, they celebrate. Those blessed with the skills and energy to do even more reach out to help other children and their families.

So, tighten your grip on your child's hand and take another step forward. Then take another and another. There's no telling how far you'll go.

Chapter Nine

Success Is a Personal Term

When you held your newborn baby in your arms, you dreamed of a happy, accomplished life for your child. You probably assumed that he or she would learn basic skills, like meaningful speech or pretend play, in the same seemingly effortless way that most children do. Now, you've learned that your child will have to work much harder than most children and may not accomplish the same things in the same way. That doesn't mean she won't be happy or won't dazzle you with her achievements. In fact, every achievement, no matter how small, may be that much sweeter. And your definition of success may be very different from your neighbor's, whether that neighbor has a typical child or one with a disability.

> He's always made constant progress. He's plateaued here and there. . . . But you could call him a success story because he really started at ground zero. Today, he is very social and he's doing well.
>
> *Brenda Eaton of Pennsylvania, mother of Brendan,*
> *now nine, diagnosed with autism at age three*

Our son's in kindergarten this year and—I would have never thought this would happen—he is not labeled with an emotional disorder. If you had told me two years ago that he'd be institutionalized, I would have believed that. I had no idea he'd be as stable as he is now.

Fred Wayne of Delaware, father of Derrick, now six, diagnosed with bipolar disorder, ADHD, and anxiety at age three

I think he's very happy for who he is and what he is and he doesn't care if other people see him differently or judge him.

Sharon Oberleitner of Idaho, mother of Robby, now eleven, diagnosed with autism at age three

His life is good because he has language. Our life is good because he has language. He's still lacking in conversation. That's not his strength. But he's working on it. . . . And he's got this great personality and a great voice.

Susan Sutherland of Massachusetts, mother of Evan, now eight, diagnosed with PDD-NOS at age three

One mother says she knew her daughter, once diagnosed with sensory integration dysfunction, had really made progress the day she went to a birthday party at a roller-skating rink. A few years earlier, this little girl could not have walked through the door of such a noisy, busy place. But that day, she rolled up to her mom after an hour of skating and said, "I like this. Can I have my next party here?"

For your child, success may mean planning her own raucous birthday parties—and, eventually, planning for college, career, and marriage. Or it may mean speaking a single word, learning to communicate by pointing at pictures, or tolerating a hug. Success may mean spending his first day, without help, in a classroom full of typical peers. Or it may mean making his first, tentative connection with one patient, talented teacher. It may mean learning to read, write, and do math. Or it may mean learning to tell a joke. One child diagnosed with a developmental disorder may someday win the school science fair; another may never win a thing, except for the hearts of all who know him.

Aim for the stars and dream of the best possible life for your child. Work as hard as you can to make that dream come true. But keep your eyes on the real prize: the child you have today.

> I have come to accept Brian for who he is. I no longer compare him to anyone other than Brian. There was a time when Brian was younger that I would become embarrassed by his lack of progress. I was always watching other children make more progress and this disheartened me. It was not good for either of us.
>
> Ann Guay of Massachusetts, mother of Brian, now
> eleven, diagnosed with autism at age three

> If you see this as a tragedy you will live a tragedy. If you see this as an opportunity in your life, if you really feel like this child is a gift in your life, you will live a gifted life.
>
> Samahria Lyte Kaufman of Massachusetts, mother
> of an adult son who recovered from autism, and co-
> founder of the Option Institute and the Son-Rise,
> Program at the Autism Treatment
> Center of America

Raising Your Child

When a baby, toddler, or preschooler first shows signs of development delay, a parent's goals are pretty clear: you must quickly have your child evaluated, diagnosed, and started in treatment. Then you watch for progress: a word, a gesture, or a golden moment of understanding and connection. As the months pass, you start thinking bigger. For many parents, the goal becomes getting their child into the most mainstream kindergarten setting possible. And, thanks to effective early intervention and more inclusive schools, many children who are diagnosed with autism and other disorders of communicating and relating will indeed attend the same schools as their typical siblings and neighbors. A few will enter kindergarten "indistinguishable from their peers," in the jargon of researchers. But many more will continue to need some help. And some children will always need intensive therapy and highly specialized help at school and at home.

In any case, many parents see kindergarten as a sort of finish line. But this is a fallacy: no one will be standing in the schoolhouse door to award your child a medal for "outstanding development" or to give you a consolation trophy for "best effort." Instead, your child will walk through that door as a small person who—just like the other small persons arriving that day—still has a lot of learning and growing to do.

As your child grows, your concerns and your goals will change, too. Even children who are doing well enough to attend a mainstream kindergarten with little or no special help often face new issues as the years pass. After all, academic and social demands increase constantly. The girl who's reading by first grade may nevertheless stumble when she's expected to read and comprehend more abstract material in third or fourth grade. The quirky boy who fits in well enough with the other five-year-olds may not be able to keep up with the subtle social maneuvering that emerges in later years.

So it's good to keep the long view in mind. Most parents can't help but worry about their child's future. But if your child isn't even in elementary school, try not to fret too much about middle school yet. Instead, think of her challenges today and in the near future. Setting goals makes sense. Early on, it may make most sense to set goals that your child might be able to reach in three to six months and certainly in no more than a year (which, not coincidentally, is the maximum time allowed between reviews of your child's Individualized Education Program).

When your child makes progress and achieves a goal, take a moment to applaud him, his teachers, his therapists, his doctors, and yourself. Then step back and think about what made that achievement possible. Was it a particular therapy or teaching approach, a medical treatment, a change in routine? Could it just be time and nature at work? You won't always be able to figure it out. But when you strongly suspect something is helping, keep it up. And keep setting new goals.

I can remember when my main goal for Sarah was that she learn to communicate her wants and needs, either with words or with gestures. A little later, my goal was to see her maintain four or five of Dr. Greenspan's "circles of communication" in a row. Sarah has long since met those goals: she is, in fact, a great communicator and can sometimes keep up a conversation—or a debate, for that matter—long enough to exhaust me. She is so skilled at logical, sustained argument that her teachers have taken to calling her "the attorney." I couldn't be prouder!

I am also constantly touched and gladdened by Sarah's obvious warmth and empathy. Not long ago, she was hosting a play date in our home for two friends about her age. A much younger girl from the neighborhood stopped by and wanted to join the fun. One of the older girls whined, "I don't want *her* to play with us." Sarah got very upset and told her friend, "Please don't say that! You're hurting her feelings."

It was the kind of moment I could only dream about when my little girl was first diagnosed.

Sarah still faces challenges—socially, emotionally, and academically. Now that's she's nine years old, I am able to take a slightly longer view. These days, my goals for Sarah are embodied in what I like to think of as a five-year "vision statement." It reads:

> Our vision for Sarah is to: (1) build and sustain "real friendships" with children in the community, based on mutual respect and acceptance; (2) expand her ability to think creatively and express herself in more logical and reflective ways; (3) continue to discover the world around her and pursue her interests; (4) keep up with her class

socially and academically with fewer supports in place;
(5) gain more self-confidence and independence as she gets
older; and (6) feel secure in the world around her.

Of course, we still have short-term goals, too. They are driven by
the longer-term vision and, always, by Sarah's ever-evolving profile
of strengths, challenges, needs, and preferences. I'll never forget the
day Sarah told me she wanted to be a cheerleader. The modern
businesswoman in me wrinkled her nose at such a girly, old-
fashioned choice. The mom in me was delighted that she wanted to
do something so thoroughly mainstream. I knew then that we were
really getting somewhere. Sarah loved cheerleading. She's also ex-
celled in gymnastics and swimming. Team sports have been harder
for her, partly because of the more complex motor planning required. Art can be tough for her, too. But she still participates in
and enjoys all these things. Other activities, such as ballet and music lessons, have fallen by the wayside. And that's okay. I introduce
Sarah to as much as possible. If she's not interested, we drop it.
She's old enough to make some of her own choices and to learn
what makes her happy.

These days, too many children, without any special needs, are
pushed to succeed in too many ways. How many children really are
cut out to be star athletes, excellent students, social butterflies, and
expert musicians, all rolled into one? Not many, I'll guess. When a
child has special needs, the pressure to be "well-rounded" and to
do exactly what everyone else is doing may be especially counter-
productive. So do what you've been doing all along: look at your
child as an individual and help her find what's right for her. Every
child needs a life outside of school and home. Every child needs a
life rich in experience. But not every child needs to play T-ball. If
your child can't or would rather not hit a ball, why not urge her to
try karate or swimming or running instead? If he makes no friends
at Cub Scouts, maybe he'll click with the members of the chess
club, the school safety patrol, the band, or the church choir. If she
hates ballet lessons but loves to draw, drop the dancing and sign

her up for a cartooning class. Not every child will have a special talent; but every child can find a passion.

Lately, Sarah has been saying that she'd like to be a rock star someday. She's already working on her act. Recently, after watching me finish a speech to a group of doctors, Sarah grabbed a little boy she'd just met—the child of one of the doctors—jumped up on the abandoned stage and started dancing and singing (into the turned-off microphone). I don't know if she'll ever win a Grammy. But she's already won the battle for a rich, imaginative life.

Telling Your Child About Her Differences

Sometime in the course of raising your child, you will face this question: just how much should you tell your child about his or her differences? This is a very personal decision. But, in general, children will benefit from an honest, matter-of-fact approach that is geared to their level of understanding and interest. Many parents find that it makes sense to answer their children's questions as they arise or become especially relevant. You certainly want to talk to your child about his challenges before he hears about them from someone else. One friend recently decided it was time to talk to her seven-year-old about the fact that he has autism. The clue appeared when she was watching a TV news report about the topic and her child ran up, turned off the set, and huffed, "I don't want to hear any more about this autism." Obviously, he had heard the word before and had some strong feelings about it!

But a six-year-old who is having trouble making friends or learning math doesn't necessarily need to know he has "Asperger syndrome" or "nonverbal learning disorder." While that information may come in handy someday—and he probably needs to know the technical terms before he reaches adolescence—for now, he probably just needs to know that you are aware of his frustration and are trying to help him. It may also help him to know that all children are different and that some things that are easy for him are hard for others. You can also help him by teaching him ways to express his needs to others—for example, to let teachers know that he needs a stretching break or a seat away from a distracting window or an especially noisy classmate.

> We use descriptive language. We try not to use labels. If she tells somebody, "I have a regulatory disorder," that's not going to help her. But if she's able to say, "I'm really feeling like I need to do some jumping," that's going to serve her much better. Besides, she doesn't know what the word "regulatory" means. She's six!
>
> *Becky Wilson of Oregon, mother of Zoë, diagnosed*
> *at age four with developmental language disorder*
> *and "regulatory disorder with autistic behaviors"*

And, of course, every child needs to know that you love them, differences and all.

> In fifth grade, my daughter asked me to come in and talk to her class about fragile X and the things that make us unique and should be celebrated. When I finished talking, I asked the children if they had questions. My daughter raised her hand. First she asked why it was so hard for her to learn and so I talked a little about that. Then she asked, "Is there a cure?" I looked at her and said, "There is nothing to cure. You are perfect the way you are."
>
> *Arlene Cohen of Michigan, mother of two children*
> *with fragile X syndrome*

My approach with Sarah has been to share information all along the way. As she's gotten older, the information has gotten more and more specific. When she tries a new medication, I tell her what it's for. When she is struggling with school or social situations, I talk about her differences and how we are working to address them. I have never hidden anything from her. But we never specifically discussed autism until one night when she was seven. That night, she came to me as I was working at my computer. "Mommy, what are you doing?" she asked. I responded, "I'm helping a parent who has a child with autism." Sarah paused for the longest moment and said, "Mommy, I have autism. That's why I go to Ann Densmore and OTA and Tomatis." Then she asked, "What is autism?" I took her in my lap and explained it to her in ways she could understand. We talked for more than an hour. I even mentioned a couple of friends from her preschool class who had autism, to which she said, matter-of-factly, "Mommy, everyone in my preschool class had autism!" She knew a lot more about her world than I ever imagined. Then, she told me that someday she hoped she could get up onstage and talk to doctors the way I do, and tell them what it's like to have autism. I told her how proud she makes me every day. It was one of the best talks we ever had.

Recently, I thought we were about to have another one of those talks. Sarah was doing her homework when, out of the blue, she blurted, "Mom, I'm going to be different for the rest of my life." My heart sank and I asked, "Why are you going to be different?" My daughter glanced up and said, "Because I'll have to wear glasses for the rest of my life!" She'd just gotten her first pair that day. I gave her a big hug and marveled at the miles we'd traveled.

It's not that Sarah has forgotten about her other challenges. She knows all about them. She will tell you that when you have autism, "it's really hard to say what you need, and you have to learn how to play with toys and other children, and sometimes you get stuck on things." She will tell you that having bipolar is awful because "you feel angry a lot." Because of her colitis, she knows she has to take pills before she can eat anything. And she knows she has to take penicillin in order to control her PANDAS and keep the rages away. Every once in a while she will ask me, "What are we working on now?" She knows that once we get her moods under control, we can begin working on her ability to focus and attend. I also have promised Sarah that as soon as the rages are gone, we will go away somewhere together on a wonderful vacation. That's something we've never been able to do successfully. Sarah has chosen a resort in the Bahamas that is famous for its "awesome water slides" and where her teen idols Mary-Kate and Ashley Olsen filmed a movie. I'd probably choose Hawaii instead, but this trip will be Sarah's reward for undergoing all these years of therapy, pills, needles, EEGs, EKGs, and IVs. She deserves it. And I can't wait to get there.

Telling Others About Your Child

Another issue that arises for most families is how much to tell other people about a child's history and challenges. These decisions can be especially tricky when a child has made significant progress. Labels and categories that described him as a toddler may no longer describe him as a grade-schooler. So why share them?

One family had a son diagnosed with an autism spectrum disorder at age two. With a good therapy program, at home and school, he made rapid progress. By first grade, his parents decided he could attend a regular private school. They let the school know the boy was receiving speech therapy but didn't share his full history. The boy's mother showed up for the first parent-teacher conference fearing her son would be "red-flagged" for special education. But the teacher only said that the boy was "a little weird." The mother was thrilled. (By the time the boy was in sixth grade, he wasn't even "a little weird anymore," says an autism program director who worked with the family.)

Often, though, the teachers and therapists at a child's school need to know his full history and developmental profile if they are to best serve him. Doctors and private therapists usually need the full story, too. Child care workers and close family members certainly need to know enough so that they can interact with your child in a positive and helpful way. Close friends also may very much want to help you and your child, but can't if they don't know about your struggles.

But what about your neighbors? Or distant relatives? Or that lady staring at your daughter in the grocery store? Again, these are highly personal matters. Some parents are very private and feel it serves their child well. Others want to share a lot of information about their child, both for the child's good and in the general belief that their openness will help to dispel the stigma that surrounds developmental disabilities.

I lean in the direction of openness. There's a wonderful little pamphlet called "At Home with Autism," produced by W. Carl Cooley, M.D., and others at the Hood Center for Family Support (Children's Hospital at Dartmouth, New Hampshire). I quote from one of the authors, a parent named Viki Gayhardt: "As parents, we've taken the first step in community involvement just by showing up with our kids, and it's an agonizing step for us to make sometimes just to go to the grocery store with our kids. . . . It's up to neighbors, parents of schoolmates, librarians, teachers, sport coaches, members of church congregations, and other community members to take that second step to keep us wanting to continue being part of society." But they can't take that second step if they don't know and understand our children.

We parents often decide on the spur of the moment how to respond to other people's questions, remarks, or apparent discomfort. One mother remembers standing in a grocery checkout line with her toddler son, who had autism, sitting in her cart. Another boy his age came up and tried to talk with him and, when he got no response, started making funny faces. The boy with autism was licking his fingers and rocking, oblivious to the other child. At first, the typical child's mother smiled at her own son's antics and then, with a visible startle, seemed to notice the other boy's unusual mannerisms. "All of a sudden she realizes the child in the basket is weird," this mother recalls. "She comes over like a maniac, grabs her son, and says, 'You stay away from him, leave that little boy alone.' " The stunned mother says she leaned over the checkout stand and said, "It's okay, it's not catching." Of course, it's entirely possible that the panicked mother of the typical child thought his behavior might be interpreted as teasing. But the disabled boy's mother felt he'd been shunned.

If your child has behavioral problems—especially if he is prone to public trantrums—it's likely that sooner or later, someone in public will criticize him or you in much blunter terms. At the very least, you will be offered well-meaning but poorly informed advice (having to do with firmer discipline, most times). If you need to physically restrain your child in public, to keep yourself or him from getting hurt, onlookers may be especially prone to misinterpret the situation. You may be deeply embarrassed. So it's probably a good idea to think ahead about what you might say at these times. I've heard that some people print up cards that explain their child has autism or another developmental disorder. I'd prefer to say something like "I'm sorry my child is annoying you but she has some medical problems that cause her to act like this." That will at least give the other person some food for thought.

I have to admit that in my own worst moment, I didn't know what to do. It was that plane ride, when Sarah was three. She raged for two hours straight as other annoyed passengers and even the flight attendants grumbled, complained, and shouted out useless advice. I wanted to get on the loudspeaker and tell them about everything my child had been through and how hard it was for our whole family. I wanted them to understand. Instead, my husband and I just sat there with tears streaming down our faces.

Of course, not everyone you encounter at a difficult moment will be cruel or ignorant. You may also encounter some wonderful kindness. One mother told of a terrible rainy afternoon when she stood in a busy parking lot struggling to get her raging five-year-old into her car. She feared that she would lose her grip on his slippery raincoat and that he'd be hit by one of the moving vehicles. Suddenly, the driver's door of a taxicab parked in the next space opened. A big man got out. He walked up, squatted down in front of the child, and said, in a deep, rich voice, "Little boy, why don't you help out your mommy and get in the car." Something about the gentleman's voice and manner got the boy's attention. He stopped screaming and quickly climbed into the car. The mother, who is not generally religious, thinks of this as the day that God himself stepped in to help her.

Your Family: Marriage Matters

No child is an island. Most live with at least one parent. The majority also have siblings. When a child has special needs, the entire family is affected. In the early days of dealing with a child's delays or disorder, when you're focused on getting help for the child in trouble, it can be difficult to think much about the impact on the rest of your family. Over time, most people start to look around at their wives, husbands, children, or other loved ones, and realize the impact. Couples suddenly realize that they haven't been out to dinner together in a year; mothers find that they haven't visited their typical child's school since they started shuttling their disabled child to therapies; fathers find themselves quietly resenting the fact that they spend Saturday mornings at special-needs swim classes instead of the soccer games everyone else seems to be attending. Money and tempers often grow short. Disappointment, guilt, and anger bubble over into hurtful arguments, or simmer silently for years.

Families in this situation face extraordinary stress, unrelenting demands, and the kinds of pressure that can break apart marriages and take a lifelong emotional toll on everyone involved. But the long-term impact might not be quite as dire as you imagine—or as you've heard. In particular, at some point you are likely to hear that 80 percent of the parents of children with disabilities end up getting divorced. That statistic pops up with great regularity on websites and TV shows. But researchers who've taken the time to try to trace this alarming number to its source have good news: *there is no study proving that the divorce rate is that high.* Some studies even suggest many marriages are strengthened by the challenges of raising a child with special needs. Robert Naseef, a Philadelphia psychologist who raised a son with severe autism and who counsels families of special-needs children, says that whenever he gives a speech to parent groups, he makes a point of dismissing this 80-percent myth. "Marriage is hard enough without thinking that yours doesn't have a chance," he says.

That said, keep in mind that about half of *all* marriages end in divorce. The divorce rate among couples with special-needs children is unlikely to be lower; it may well be higher, though studies have yet to prove this. It is clear, however, that families of disabled children face more and different challenges. How they handle these challenges has a profound impact on how the family functions and on whether relationships within the family thrive or fail. The secrets to success remain somewhat elusive, though. In their book *Ordinary Families, Special Children,* the psychologist Milton Seligman and the sociologist Rosalyn Benjamin Darling put it this way: "Although the data regarding marital satisfaction and divorce in families of children with disabilities are contradictory, we do know that some marriages are under stress but remain intact, others simply fail, while still others survive and are even enhanced. Our task should probably be to understand why some families disintegrate while others thrive."

> The effect is devastating. It brings out the worst in both of us, and the marriage is shaky. My husband is desperate because he doesn't know how long he can keep up the hours (at work), and I'm desperate to get Noah into a program so I can get back to work, so that my husband can cut back his hours.
>
> *Karin Cather of Virginia, mother of two boys with autism spectrum disorders*

> It has definitely affected our marriage, as we don't have alone time and very few opportunities to go out alone for dinner or see friends, so our social life has taken a nosedive. But it has also strengthened our bond, as we spend a lot of

time together and want the same things for our son and our family.

Susan Sutherland of Massachusetts, mother of Evan,
diagnosed with PDD-NOS at age three

My marriage is especially strong now after all the obstacles we have overcome.

Ida Palmieri of New Jersey, mother of Michael,
diagnosed with autism at age two

Experts do agree that having a special needs child is unlikely to save a marriage that otherwise would fail. Sometimes, the initial crisis may postpone a breakup, though. One woman whose son has autism remembers that when he was young, she and her husband worked as a precision team. "We took turns so that the other one would get a break. One would escape out the front door while the other one would entertain my son so he wouldn't have a tantrum because someone was leaving the house. . . . We were on duty 24-7." After a few years, the couple's son greatly improved. With the crisis past, the marriage failed, a victim of "preexisting conditions," the mother says. "We had put all of our differences aside because we knew we had to focus on what he needed. Once our son started doing better, the issues came back."

My own marriage simply failed, for reasons that likely existed before our daughter was born. In our crisis, my husband and I were not able to work together. I put all my time and effort into helping Sarah. He wanted me to put more time and effort into our marriage. I wanted him to put more time and effort into Sarah. The final straw was financial, as it is in many marriages, whether or not the family includes children with special needs. In the end, we just could not live together. I'm sad for Sarah that it worked out that way.

I certainly am not an expert on saving a marriage in crisis. But counselors who work with parents of special-needs children give couples consistent advice:

Second Steps and Beyond **213**

- Find time to spend together. Work hard to find a babysitter so that you can get a date night. Or have a date at home, with a nice dinner, a glass of wine, and a grown-up conversation, even if you have to wait until the kids are asleep to do it.
- Let your spouse know how much you appreciate all he or she does.
- Tell your spouse when you need help. Likewise, be alert to signs that your spouse needs help and support.
- Share your feelings, even if they include anger and guilt. And listen to your partner's feelings, even if they differ from yours.
- When you find yourselves unable to communicate and find solutions, seek professional help.

Counselors who work with such couples say some common issues arise. And often, though not always, fathers and mothers divide along predictable lines. Dads often feel overwhelmed by the financial strain, and may feel that their most important contribution is to hold a job and pay the bills. Or they may deeply wish to participate directly in their child's care and therapy, but complain that their wives criticize their efforts or shut them out. And they often feel abandoned by wives who are focusing almost entirely on their children's needs. For their part, mothers often feel overwhelmed by the day-to-day responsibility to care for their children and arrange treatment and schooling. Some feel that their spouses are insufficiently appreciative or too critical of their efforts. Women also may feel more pressure than men do to cut back or quit their jobs—and more guilt if they can't do so, or choose not to.

Tension between parents obviously puts a strain on marriages. It can also affect a child's care. A Michigan psychologist, Dr. Ira Glovinsky, did an informal study of parents seeking his help for young children with severe mood disorders. He divided the parents into three groups. In the first, both parents came to every appointment and were highly involved and supportive of each other. In the second, the mothers were much more involved than the fathers, and the fathers "generally dismissed the idea that there was a serious problem." The third group was composed of single mothers. He found that children of the parents who worked closely together progressed most rapidly—and that the second-best progress was seen in the children of single mothers. "When the parents were in disagreement, it set up a real negative cycle and paralyzed the mothers because the fathers rejected everything they tried to do," Glovinsky says.

Of course, sometimes fathers are the parents who are more alert to their children's needs and more aggressive about seeking help. Sometimes they take the lead in their child's care, even quitting their jobs and giving up income, with little support from their spouses. In either case, parents who are constantly at odds, over their children's care or other issues, aren't providing an ideal home for anyone.

None of which is to say that becoming—or remaining—a single parent is ideal. Parents who are raising their children alone face extra difficulties. The biggest difference is that getting a break can be much harder. Forget about "date night." I could use a half hour alone to take a bubble bath! Though I love spending time with my daughter and I want to devote this part of my life to her, I know I also need more time by myself and with other adults. And it's almost impossible to get that. I have wonderful babysitters who look after my daughter when I must travel for First Signs, and Sarah spends one weekend a month with her dad. But most days, it's just Sarah and me. My mother and stepfather are wonderful and help out whenever they can, but as they get older they are finding it more and more difficult to care for Sarah. Recently, a woman who was helping me to respond to e-mails answered one from a woman who wanted to know how she could help her sister, who has a child with autism. The response was so perfect: "If you are there to listen, to laugh, and to cry with her, you are giving her a very big gift. You may also want to provide her with some respite that she most likely desperately needs. Just an evening here and there to allow your sister a chance to do something for herself would be a great gift."

You need great family. You probably need a counselor. And you need really great friends.

Debra Egan of New Jersey, single mother of Gabi,
diagnosed with autism at eighteen months

Your Family: Sibling Support

If you have more than one child, you have an additional concern: how will having a disabled sibling affect your other children?

The short answer is that the effects can be both positive and negative. Siblings of children with special needs report that they feel anger, guilt, shame, and confusion about their siblings' differences. They sometimes feel that their parents neglect them or expect too much of them, because they are the "normal ones." They sometimes expect too much of themselves and try to make up for their siblings' problems by being perfect themselves. They worry about how much responsibility they will have to take for their siblings as adults. Young children worry that they will catch a sibling's disability; young adults worry that they will pass the disorder on to their own children. But these brothers and sisters also say they feel pride in the hard-won accomplishments of their disabled siblings and in their own ability to help their siblings make progress. Some say they are more tolerant, patient, and mature because of their experiences growing up with a disabled sibling. Many report their families are especially close and loving.

From the moment our special needs siblings are diagnosed, we must deal with the fact that we will never get as much attention as them. . . . Later in life, after our parents have passed away, we alone must bear the burden of taking care of our special-needs siblings. Yet, the irony is, the fact that I am the sibling of a special-needs child is the very thing that enables me to bear the load I am burdened with. Living in a family that has to deal with the problems autism creates has made me a strong, independent person. I will always be tied to my family in a way that other children are not.

Katherine Flaschen, sixteen, of Massachusetts, sister
of a fourteen-year-old with autism

My seven-year-old son is good to his brother but gets easily frustrated. Last year his brother had a snow day and his school opened. He asked me why autistic kids get everything. Ouch.

Ann Guay of Massachusetts, mother of three,
including a boy with autism

Many parents report that their other children get great satisfaction out of being role models for their siblings with disabilities. One mom says her highly social, imaginative toddler son was so determined to make a playmate out of his older sister, who had an autism spectrum disorder, that he became "a natural therapist" for her. He insisted she play with him. And it worked: the two now play together every day. Another mother says her older son ignored his brother with autism for years, probably out of anxiety and fear. Today, at age ten, he loves playing with his seven-year-old brother and showing him all the things he thinks a boy should know, from video games to tree-climbing.

You can't dictate how your typical children feel about your child with a disability. Family counselors usually give parents the following advice.

- Tell siblings the truth about their brother or sister, in terms they can understand. Very young children can understand that a sibling needs help with speaking or playing. Elementary school children can understand that their sibling has a disorder and needs special education and therapy to improve. Teenagers can understand the fine details of their sibling's disorder and implications for adulthood.

- Give siblings permission and opportunity to express their feelings, including anger and embarrassment. Never tell your typical child that he "should not" feel the way he does; instead, help him understand his feelings and how he can cope.

- Consider individual therapy or a support group for siblings who are struggling with their feelings. Many communities also participate in a program called Sibshops, a series of workshops in which siblings of disabled children spend a few hours having fun together and talking about their families. Online groups for siblings can also help.

- Help siblings find satisfying ways to interact with one another. If a child wants to help his disabled sibling, show him how. If he finds interacting with his sibling too difficult, respect his need to back away, but work on ways to eventually bridge the gap.

- Expect your typical child to tease and fight with his disabled sibling; that's normal behavior among all brothers and sisters. Handle squabbles in a low-key, fair manner. An overreaction can cause your typical child needless guilt.

- Celebrate the accomplishments and recognize the challenges faced by each child. Typical children can have emotional and academic difficulties, too. They also have hard-won accomplishments and need your praise just as much as your disabled child does. Be alert to the needs of all your children.

- Expect all of your children to participate in family life to their fullest ability. If your disabled child can perform simple chores, assign them. If he can be taught basic good manners—like staying at the table until the end of a meal—teach them. You'll help establish a sense of fairness and also better prepare all of your children for the most independent adult lives possible.

- Find ways to do things together as a family. If everyone can't go to a movie theater, maybe everyone can go to the zoo. If you can't all go to restaurants, go on picnics, even if you have to start by holding them in your backyard.
- Spend time alone with each child, doing things that he or she enjoys. It doesn't have to be much: a weekly fast-food lunch or a walk through the mall can give you time to connect with a typical child. And don't feel guilty about leaving your special-needs child out of an activity—a trip to an amusement park, say, or a day of laser tag—that might be no fun for him at all.

> Whenever I hear a parent say, "I treat my disabled child just like my other children," I say, "Oh, boy, we need to talk."
> *Samahria Lyte Kaufman of Massachusetts, mother of an adult son recovered from autism and co-founder of the Option Institute and the Son-Rise Program at the Autism Treatment Center of America*

Every child is unique, so his or her needs are unique. That's true for children with disabilities. It's true for their brothers and sisters, too. And always remember that parents are the best teachers for all of their children, disabled and not.

> If the parents perceive this as a life-searing tragedy from which there is no escape, they shouldn't be surprised if their children see it that way, too. If they see it as a series of challenges that are difficult but that they can face with grace and humor, they have every reason to believe that their children will see it that way, too.
> *Don Meyer, director of the Sibling Support Project of the Arc of the United States*

To Do Now

Every parent should have a will. If you are the parent of a child with special needs, it's especially important that you make plans for that child in the event of your death.

Such planning falls into two categories: people and money.

First, you need to think about who would take care of your child if you died tomorrow. Have a frank conversation now with that person, and find out if they are willing and able to take on the challenge of raising a child with a disability. Consider their age, health, and other commitments and pick someone both enthusiastic and well prepared for the job. Sometimes even our children may ponder this topic. Recently, Sarah came to me and asked, "Mommy, if you die who will make the autism go away?" Nothing hits home harder than a question like that.

Second, you need to think about money. Simply leaving your assets to your child may be a mistake. If your child ends up with a significant, lifelong disability, he or she will be eligible for certain kinds of government assistance—aid that may be denied if your adult child has his or her own assets. Consult an attorney to find out how to set up a "special needs trust" that will assure your child is well cared for, even in your absence.

Chapter Ten

Parents as Advocates

Every parent becomes an advocate. It's part of the basic job description. We all try to get what our children need, from our schools and communities and from the individual teachers, coaches, child care workers, doctors, and others who can help shape our children's futures. Many parents become advocates for children in a larger sense. They join PTAs and neighborhood watches; they fight for a cleaner environment, a safer world, a more wholesome culture, and a more workable, affordable health care system.

When your child has a developmental disorder, you have no choice but to advocate for your child's individual needs. Advocacy is your Job One.

By the time your child has a diagnosis and you have taken the first steps toward his treatment and education, you may indeed be an expert advocate. That's a good thing. You are going to need your newly sharpened skills for years to come. The fight for your child's future is just beginning. And, as you continue to fight for your child, you may find yourself wondering: What else can I do—not only for my child, but for others with developmental disabilities? As many parents have learned, there's a lot of work to be done. If you are willing and able, you might help change the world for your child and for millions of others.

It's not fair what my family and I have had to go through, and no one should have to follow the same path. One child hit by autism is one child too many.

Joy Johnson of Maryland, mother of two boys
with autism

Individual Advocacy

For most parents, the most pressing concerns will continue to be those that directly affect their children. The yearly—or more frequent—IEP meetings. The ongoing, endless battles with insurers. The search for doctors, therapists, consultants, adequate child care. As your child grows, you will find yourself in constant negotiation with the agencies and people who provide your family services and support. Just remember these guiding principles:

- Know your child. All children change. Some with developmental disorders change radically from year to year, due to the effects of treatment and the complex nature of neurological disorders. Some develop new problems and get new diagnoses. Others make so much progress that old labels no longer apply. Keep track of these changes with the same diligence you applied to getting your child an initial diagnosis. That means having him reevaluated from time to time, not only by the school system but by private practitioners. And it means paying attention to your child, spending time with him at home, observing him at school and at play, and knowing him better than anyone else.
- Know the services. School systems change their policies and programs all the time. The best doctors and therapists constantly reevaluate their techniques, learning about new treatments and methods and discarding outmoded or discredited ones. New practitioners come to a community; others leave. You should know almost as much about

these changes as the professionals do, and sometimes more. Attend school meetings. Sign up for conferences about new treatment methods. Check out new providers in your community. And stay abreast of the lively discussion—in medical journals, online boards, and at scientific meetings—about best treatment practices.

- Know your rights. Laws about special education, disability rights, and health care change frequently. Keep up with the changes. Not every parent of a child with special needs will have to hire a lawyer to get what her child requires, but remember that seeking professional legal advice is always an option.

For many parents, their toughest assignment will continue to be working with schools. If you are very lucky, you will meet someone like Angela Jervey, the principal of the school Sarah attended from kindergarten through second grade. We worked together as a team and she saw that Sarah (and all the other children) had the services and supports they needed. She is a special lady who is deeply committed to every child and teacher at the Sweetsir School. When I told her I was writing this book, I asked her about her philosophy. She said: "All children have a right to belong. 'Fair' is getting what the child needs. . . . I love the parents who put the child's picture on the table when we come together. All the decisions made should be based on the child and what the child needs. This is why we are here."

But opinions about what a child needs can vary widely. Some parents and educators believe that all children, no matter what their disabilities, should be with typical peers all or most of the time. They believe this is best for children with disabilities and for typical children, because they all learn from one another. Such "full inclusion" is increasingly common and is supported by a federal special education law that says children should be educated in the "least restrictive" environments possible. That means children with special needs are not automatically placed in traditional, separate, special education classrooms. Many now spend the day in mainstream classrooms, accompanied by aides.

But special education classrooms have not disappeared. In fact, many parents and educators continue to believe they are the best choice for some children who need intense, individualized attention through much of the school day. The difference is that many children assigned to these classrooms today divide their time between their small special-needs classrooms and mainstream classes. Almost all are included with typical children for part of the day, even if it's just for lunch and recess.

Some children—usually those with moderate to severe physical and/or mental disabilities—still attend separate, special schools. Again, parents who make this choice believe it is best for their children.

The decisions can be agonizing. One mom, whose eleven-year-old son with autism attends a private special-needs school, says she once wanted to transfer him to a public school with typical children. Her husband disagreed. The disagreement about school soon turned into a painful broader discussion. The woman's husband suggested she was treating their son "like a broken car" that could be fixed with the right combination of treatments and educational techniques, and that putting him in a typical classroom would give her a sense of achievement, but do nothing for their child. His words hurt but rang true, she says: "It was a real turning point for me. Up until that point, I had hoped for a cure. Autism was merely a temporary way station for me, not forever." She agreed to keep her son in the private school, a decision that she now feels was right for him and has allowed him to make the most progress possible.

Another mother who has always kept her eighteen-year-old son with autism in inclusive classrooms is just as happy with her family's choice. Her son, she says, strongly prefers to be around typical teens and constantly learns from the people around him. "He sees himself far more in the typical world than in the atypical world. And probably we're at fault. We've encouraged that."

Deciding where your child belongs on this continuum—and

developing a personal philosophy about the societal value of inclusion is a job for individual parents. But part of your job as an advocate for your child is also making sure that schools always follow the law, that they start with the assumption that your child will be educated alongside her peers, to the fullest extent possible. If you decide inclusion isn't possible or appropriate for your child, you have the right to other choices.

Reaching Out

For many parents, a mission to help their own children quickly turns into a desire to help other children as well. Most start small, sharing advice with other parents at support groups and online. Many go on to help families throughout their communities or beyond.

It was very clear to me when Max was young that the only way I was going to survive his disability was to become empowered and to become knowledgeable, both professionally and personally. . . . But it wasn't enough for me to focus just on him. I wanted to share the wealth.

Gail Tino of Massachusetts, mother of an eighteen-year-old with autism

I have met and heard about many parents who, like me, ended up changing their careers as a result of their child's diagnosis and their experiences with the health care and education systems. One successful lawyer quit her lucrative practice to become an unpaid advocate for other parents struggling with their schools. Many parents have jettisoned other interests to become professional therapists, special education teachers, consultants, or classroom aides. Other fathers and mothers have started organizations or taken positions in existing organizations that advocate for children with disabilities. Still others volunteer their precious time to answer phones or file papers for worthy organizations.

There was a point where I had gone to a hundred autism conferences. I had a master's in nursing. I knew I could help other people. Now I'm a behavior analyst and work in classrooms all around Pennsylvania.

Mary Barbera, mother of eight-year-old Lucas

I felt like we were lucky and we needed to give something back. I didn't want anyone else to be told that their child would never speak.

Kathy Bauer of Pennsylvania, mother of two
children with speech apraxia and spokeswoman
for Apraxia-Kids

For me, this work has been exhilarating and life-changing. I know I am doing something that matters. It's true that, between First Signs and caring for Sarah, I have given up any sort of normal social life or leisure. But the people I meet and talk to each day, the professionals and parents working so hard for all of our children, more than fill the gap. These are incredibly passionate, committed people. I am proud to know them.

And there is so much to do. Right now, organizations in the vanguard are fighting for

- laws that will require insurers to pay for developmental screening and treatments for developmental disorders
- funding for research that will establish the causes and point to more effective treatments for autism and related disorders
- increased public awareness of the signs of developmental delay
- increased public awareness of the needs of children and adults with autism and other developmental disorders
- better-funded, more accountable special education programs

- better job and housing opportunities for adults with developmental disabilities

Of course not everyone has the skill, desire, or opportunity to become a professional advocate. Most parents, especially those raising a child with a disability, are struggling every day just to do the things they must do for their own families, caring for their children, holding down jobs, keeping their households afloat.

But everyone can do something. Here are a few ways to get involved:

- Join a local chapter of a group that advocates for children like yours. If one doesn't exist, start one. Linking with others can help make your voice heard, even if you can contribute only a little time or money.
- Join the parent advisory council for your local school district. If you don't have the time or energy to join, at least attend some meetings and make your views known.
- Show up for school board meetings when special education policies are on the agenda. Get to know the players and fight for the best programs for your child and others.
- Lobby your school system for better training and higher pay for special education teachers and aides.
- Volunteer at your child's school, even if you can only make it one hour a week. Whether you supervise the lunchroom, make copies in the office, or help directly in the classroom, you'll be making an important contribution.
- Become a mentor for other parents in your community's Early Intervention program or your school system.
- Educate your employer about the needs of families raising children with developmental disorders. This is especially valuable if you work for a company that runs its own health insurance program and has the power to make positive changes.

- Invite treatment experts to your community to hold work-shops and seminars for parents and educators.
- Participate in fund-raisers. When your local organization holds a walkathon, golf tournament, or casino night, give whatever time and money you can.

We all have to work together and find out what's needed because there is an epidemic going on.

Sharon Oberleitner of Idaho, mother of an eleven-year-old boy with autism

Parents who get involved this way see a great fringe benefit: they meet more parents of children with developmental disorders. As one father says, "Any time you get families together, whether it's for a conference, a walkathon, or a fund-raising dinner, it becomes a little bit of a support group. In between courses of dinner, we're all talking about our kids and their therapies and what we've done that works."

But you can't change the world by talking only with people who share your experiences and views. So get out there. Talk to people. Make sure they know your child's story, and make sure they know how many families are struggling with autism and other developmental disorders. You may find that some people who should know the facts really have no idea. One couple recently met with the director of their synagogue's religious school to talk about creating a modified program for their seven-year-old son, who has autism. The director was warm and welcoming, but said she'd only been asked twice before in twelve years to enroll a child with significant special needs. This was a temple serving several hundred families. Where were the other children with developmental disorders? The director had assumed they did not exist; the parents knew otherwise. They now hope to start a special education program at their synagogue—not only for their son, but for the other children who might come if only they were invited.

So be brave about taking your child out to meet the world. If you can, take him to libraries, restaurants, swimming pools, grocery stores, and places of worship. That's often difficult, especially when a child has behavioral problems or obvious differences that prompt stares and questions. But err on the side of sunshine: no child should live his life in the shadows.

Awareness is hugely important. Everyone has to be willing to talk about it, to tell their friends, to tell their work colleagues. There's no good explanation for why we now have one in 166 kids with autism except that it's growing. And unless we do something soon, it could get worse.

Peter Bell, executive director of Cure Autism Now
and father of a boy with autism

As for me, I'm going to continue the fight on all fronts. Every day, when I wake my daughter, I will think of what I can do that day to make her life a little better, her future a little brighter. Every day, I'll also be thinking of your sons and daughters—and fighting for the future all children deserve.

Bibliography

Accardo, Pasquale J., M.D., and Barbara Y. Whitman, with Carla Laszewski, Carol A. Haake, and Jill D. Morrow. *Dictionary of Developmental Disabilities Terminology.* Baltimore, Md.: Brookes Publishing Company, 2002.

American Academy of Child and Adolescent Psychiatry. *Your Child: Emotional, Behavioral, and Cognitive Development from Birth Through Preadolescence.* New York: HarperResource, 2000.

American Academy of Pediatrics, Committee on Children with Disabilities. "Policy Statement: Developmental Surveillance and Screening of Infants and Young Children." *Pediatrics* 108 (2001), 192–95.

————. "Policy Statement: The Pediatrician's Role in the Diagnosis and Management of Autistic Spectrum Disorders in Children." *Pediatrics* 107 (2001), 1221–26.

American Psychiatric Association. *Diagnostic and Statistical Manual of Mental Disorders,* 4th ed. (text revision). Washington, D.C., 2000.

Bagnato, Stephen J., John T. Neisworth, and Susan M. Munson. *Linking Assessment and Early Intervention: An Authentic Curriculum-Based Approach.* Baltimore, Md.: Brookes Publishing Company, 1996.

Boyle, C. A., P. Decoufle, and M. Yeargin-Allsopp. "Prevalence and

Health Impact of Developmental Disabilities in U.S. Children."
Pediatrics 9 (1994), 399–403.

Dobos, A. E., P. H. Dworkin, and B. Bernstein. "Pediatricians'
Approaches to Developmental Problems: Has the Gap Been
Narrowed?" *Journal of Developmental and Behavioral Pediatrics* 15
(1994), 34–39.

Dworkin, P. H. "Detection of Behavioral, Developmental, and
Psychosocial Problems in Pediatric Primary Care Practice." *Current
Opinions in Pediatrics* 5 (1993), 531–36.

Filipek, P. A., P. J. Accardo, G. T. Baranek, E. H. Cook, G. Dawson, B.
Gordon, J. S. Gravel, C. P. Johnson, R. J. Kallen, S. E. Levy, N. J.
Minshew, B. M. Prizant, I. Rapin, S. J. Rogers, W. L. Stone, S. Teplin,
R. F. Tuchman, and F. R. Volkmar. "The Screening and Diagnosis of
Autistic Spectrum Disorders." *Journal of Autism and Developmental
Disorders* 29 (1999), 439–84.

———, P. J. Accardo, S. Ashwal, G. T. Baranek, E. H. Cook, Jr.,
G. Dawson, B. Gordon, J. S. Gravel, C. P. Johnson, R. J. Kallen, S. E.
Levy, N. J. Minshew, S. Ozonoff, B. M. Prizant, I. Rapin, S. J. Rogers,
W. L. Stone, S. W. Teplin, R. F. Tuchman, and F. R. Volkmar. "Practice
Parameter: Screening and Diagnosis of Autism." *Neurology* 55 (2000),
468–79.

First Signs, Inc. "First Signs Guide to Developmental and Autism
Screening Tools." Merrimac, Mass.: First Signs, Inc., 2001.

———. *On the Spectrum: Children and Autism* (video). Available from
First Signs, Inc., P.O. Box 358, Merrimac, MA 01860.

———. First Signs Screening Kit for Pediatric Professionals. Merrimac,
Mass.: First Signs, Inc., 2001.

———. "Is Your Baby Meeting These Important Milestones? Key Social,
Emotional, Communication, and Behavior Milestones for Your Baby's
Healthy Development" (Greenspan, Prizant, Wetherby, First Signs,
Inc.). Note: The milestones were compiled and adapted with
permission from the following sources: S. I. Greenspan, *Building
Healthy Minds* (Reading, Mass.: Perseus Books, 2001); B. M. Prizant,
A. M. Wetherby, and J. E. Roberts, "Communication Problems" (in C.
Zeanah, ed., *Handbook of Infant Mental Health*, 2nd ed. [New York:

Guilford Press, 2000]), and A. M. Wetherby, *Babies Learn to Talk at an Amazing Rate*, FIRST WORDS Project, Florida State University.

Flaschen, K. "Family Bond." *The Autism Perspective (TAP)* 1 (2005), 78.

Gabovitch, E. M., and N. D. Wiseman. "Early Identification of Autism Spectrum Disorders." In D. Zager, *Autism: Identification, Education and Treatment*, 3rd. ed. (Mahwah, N.J.: Erlbaum, 2004), 145–72.

Gill, Barbara. *Changed by a Child: Companion Notes for Parents of a Child with a Disability.* Warner, N.H.: Mainstreet Books, 1998.

Glascoe, F. P. "Are Over-referrals on Developmental Screening Tests Really a Problem?" *Archives of Pediatric and Adolescent Medicine* 155 (2001), 54–59.

———. *Collaborating with Parents: Using Parents' Evaluation of Developmental Status to Detect and Address Developmental and Behavioral Problems.* Nashville, Tenn.: Ellsworth & Vandermeer, 1998.

———. "Do Parental Characteristics Influence the Accuracy of Their Developmental and Behavioral Concerns?" Presentation to the Ambulatory Pediatric Association Annual Meeting, May 1994. *Archives of Pediatric and Adolescent Medicine* 148 (1994), 80.

———. "Early Detection of Developmental Problems." *Pediatrics in Review* 21 (2000), 272–80.

———. "Parents' Evaluation of Developmental Status" (PEDS). Nashville, Tenn.: Ellsworth & Vandermeer, 1997.

———. "Using Parents' Concerns to Detect and Address Developmental and Behavioral Problems." *Journal of the Society of Pediatric Nurses* 4 (1999), 24–35.

———, F. M. Foster, and M. L. Wolraich. "An Economic Evaluation of Four Methods for Detecting Developmental Problems." *Pediatrics* 99 (1997), 830–37.

———, K. E. Byrne, B. Chang, B. Strickland, L. Ashford, and K. Johnson. "The Accuracy of the Denver-II in Developmental Screening." *Pediatrics* 89 (1992), 1221–25.

———, P. Sievers, and N. D. Wiseman. "First Signs Model Program Makes Great Strides in Early Detection in Minnesota: Clinicians Play Major Role in Increased Screenings." *Developmental and Behavioral News* 13 (2) (Fall 2004), 20–22.

Gracious, B. L., E. A. Youngstrom, R. L. Findling, and J. R. Calabrese. "Discriminative Validity of a Parent Version of the Young Mania Rating Scale." *American Academy of Child and Adolescent Psychiatry* 41 (11) (November 2002), 1350–59.

Greenspan, S. I. *Infancy and Early Childhood: The Practice of Clinical Assessment and Intervention with Emotional and Developmental Challenges.* Madison, Conn.: International Universities Press, 1992.

———, with Nancy Breslau Lewis. *Building Healthy Minds: The Six Experiences That Create Intelligence and Emotional Growth in Babies and Young Children.* Cambridge Mass.: Perseus, 2000.

———, with Nancy Thorndike Greenspan. *First Feelings: Milestones in the Emotional Development of Your Child.* New York: Penguin Books, 1994.

———, and S. Shanker. *The First Idea: How Symbols, Language and Intelligence Evolved from Our Primate Ancestors to Modern Humans.* Cambridge, Mass.: Perseus, 2004.

———, and Serena Wieder. *The Child with Special Needs: Encouraging Intellectual and Emotional Growth.* Cambridge, Mass.: Perseus, 1998.

Guralnick, Michael J. *The Effectiveness of Early Intervention.* Baltimore, Md.: Brookes Publishing Company, 1996.

Hallowell, Edward, M.D. *When You Worry About the Child You Love: A Reassuring Guide to Solving Your Child's Emotional and Learning Problems.* New York: Fireside, 1997.

Lord, C., and J. McGee, eds. *Educational Interventions for Children with Autism Educating Children with Autism.* Washington, D.C.: National Academy Press, 2001.

Martin, Nicholas. *Strengthening Relationships When Our Children Have Special Needs.* Arlington, Tex.: Future Horizons, 2004.

Morse, Danielle, Viki Gayhardt, and R. Stuart Wallace. *At Home with Autism. Three Families' Stories.* Stratham, N.H.: Potential Unlimited Publishing, 1998.

Neisworth, John T., and Pamela S. Wolfe. *The Autism Encyclopedia.* Baltimore, Md.: Brookes Publishing Company, 2005.

Osterling, J., and G. Dawson. "Early Recognition of Children with Autism: A Study of First Birthday Home Videotapes." *Journal of Autism and Developmental Disorders* 24 (1994), 247–57.

Palfrey J. S., J. D. Singer, D. K. Walker, and J. A. Butler. "Early Identification of Children's Special Needs: A Study in Five Metropolitan Communities." *Journal of Pediatrics* 111 (1994), 651–55.

Prizant, B. M., A. M. Wetherby, and J. E. Roberts. "Communication Problems." In C. Zeanah, ed., *Handbook of Infant Mental Health*, 2nd ed. New York: Guilford Press, 2000.

Ratey, John J., M.D., and Catherine Johnson. *Shadow Syndromes: The Mild Forms of Major Mental Disorders That Sabotage Us*. New York: Bantam, 1998.

Robins, D., D. Fein, M. Barton, and J. Green. "The Modified Checklist for Autism in Toddlers (M-CHAT): An Initial Study Investigating the Early Detection of Autism and Pervasive Developmental Disorders." *Journal of Autism and Developmental Disorders* 31 (2001), 131–44.

———, D. Fein, M. Barton, G. Jones, J. Byrne, M. Hinchey, and J. LeBlanc. *The M-CHAT: Early Detection of Autism*. Storrs, Conn.: University of Connecticut Press, 1999.

———, D. Fein, J. Kleinman, P. Dixon, G. Marshia, S. Allen, and M. Barton. "The Modified Checklist for Autism in Toddlers (M-CHAT) Detects Autism Spectrum Disorders in 2-Year-Old Children." Paper presented at the Society for Research in Child Development, Tampa, Fla. (April 2003).

Sears, William, M.D., and Martha Sears. *The Baby Book: Everything You Need to Know About Your Child from Birth to Age 2*. New York: Little, Brown, 2003.

Seligman, M., and R. B. Darling. *Ordinary Families, Special Children: A Systems Approach to Childhood Disability*, 2nd ed. New York: Guilford Press, 1999.

Shonkoff, Jack P., and Samuel J. Meisels. *Handbook of Early Childhood Intervention*. Cambridge: Cambridge University Press, 2000.

Shonkoff, J. P., and D. A. Phillips. *From Neurons to Neighborhoods: The Science of Early Childhood Development*. Washington, D.C.: National Research Council, Committee on Integrating the Science of Early Childhood Development, 2000.

Stacey, Patricia. *The Boy Who Loved Windows: Opening the Heart and Mind of a Child Threatened with Autism*. Cambridge, Mass.: Da Capo Press, 2003.

Wetherby, A. M. *Babies Learn to Talk at an Amazing Rate*. Tallahassee: Florida State University FIRST WORDS Project, 1999.

———, and B. M. Prizant. 2002 Communication and Symbolic Behavior Scales (CSBS) Developmental Profile (First Normed Edition). Baltimore, Md.: Paul H. Brookes Publishing.

Woolf, Alan D., M.D., Howard Shane, Ph.D., and Margaret Kenna, M.D. *The Children's Hospital Guide to Your Child's Health and Development*. New York: Perseus, 2002.

Zigler, Edward F., Matia Finn-Stevenson, and Nancy W. Hall. *The First Three Years and Beyond: Brain Development and Social Policy*. New Haven: Yale University Press, 2002.

Recommended Reading

Anderson, W., S. Chitwood, and D. Hayden. *Negotiating the Special Education Maze: A Guide for Parents and Teachers*, 3rd ed. Bethesda, Md.: Woodbine House, 1997.

Ayres, A. Jean. *Sensory Integration and the Child*. Los Angeles: Western Psychological Services, 1979.

Batshaw, Mark L. *Children with Disabilities*. Baltimore, Md.: Brookes Publishing Company, 2002.

———. *When Your Child Has a Disability: The Complete Sourcebook of Daily and Medical Care*. Baltimore, Md.: Brookes Publishing Company, 2000.

Brazelton, T. Berry, M.D. *Infants and Mothers: Differences in Development*. New York: Dell, 1983.

———. *Touchpoints Three to Six: Your Child's Behavioral and Emotional Development*. Cambridge, Mass.: Perseus, 2002.

———. *Touchpoints: Your Child's Emotional and Behavioral Development, Birth–3*. Cambridge, Mass.: Da Capo Press, 1992.

———, and Stanley I. Greenspan, M.D. *The Irreducible Needs of Children: What Every Child Must Have to Grow, Learn, and Flourish*. Cambridge, Mass.: Perseus, 2001.

Cutler, Barbara Coyne. *You, Your Child, and "Special" Education: A Guide to Making the System Work*. Baltimore, Md.: Brookes Publishing Company, 1995.

Eisenberg, Arlene, Heidi E. Murkoff, and Sandee E. Hathaway, B.S.N. *What to Expect: The Toddler Years.* New York: Workman, 1994, 1996.

Fouse, Beth. *Creating a Win-Win IEP for Students with Autism.* Arlington, Tex.: Future Horizons, 1999.

Garcia, W. Joseph. *Sign with Your Baby: How to Communicate with Infants Before They Can Speak,* revised ed. Seattle, Wash.: Northlight Communications, 2002.

Greenspan, Stanley I., M.D., with Nancy Thorndike Greenspan. *First Feelings: Milestones in the Emotional Development of Your Child.* New York: Penguin Books, 1994.

————, with Nancy Breslau Lewis. *Building Healthy Minds: The Six Experiences That Create Intelligence and Emotional Growth in Babies and Young Children.* Cambridge, Mass.: Perseus, 2000.

————, and Serena Wieder. *The Child with Special Needs: Encouraging Intellectual and Emotional Growth.* Cambridge, Mass.: Perseus, 1998.

Kaufman, Barry Neil. *Son-Rise: The Miracle Continues.* Novato, Calif.: New World Library, 1995.

Klass, Perri, M.D., and Eileen Costello. *Quirky Kids: Understanding and Helping Your Child Who Doesn't Fit In—When to Worry and When Not to Worry.* New York: Ballantine Books, 2003.

Kranowitz, Carol Stock, M.A. *The Out-of-Sync Child: Recognizing and Coping with Sensory Integration Dysfunction.* New York: Perigee Books, 1998.

Leach, Penelope, M.D. *Your Baby and Child: From Birth to Age Five.* New York: Knopf, 1997.

Lovaas, Ivar O. *Teaching Individuals with Developmental Delays: Basic Intervention Techniques.* Austin, Tex.: Pro-Ed, 2002.

Maurice, Catherine. *Let Me Hear Your Voice: A Family's Triumph Over Autism.* New York: Ballantine Books, 1994.

————, Gina Green, and Stephen C. Luce, eds. *Behavioral Intervention for Young Children with Autism: A Manual for Parents and Professionals.* Austin, Tex.: Pro-Ed, 1996.

Murkoff, Heidi, Arlene Eisenberg, and Sandee Hathaway, B.S.N. *What to Expect the First Year.* New York: Workman, 1989, 1986, 2003.

Naseef, Robert A., Ph.D. *Special Children, Challenged Parents.* Baltimore, Md.: Brookes Publishing Company, 2001.

Papolos, D. F., M.D., and J. Papolos. *The Bipolar Child: The Definitive and Reassuring Guide to Childhood's Most Misunderstood Disorder.* New York: Broadway Books, 2002.

Powell, Thomas, and Peggy Ahrenhold Gallagher. *Brothers & Sisters—A Special Part of Exceptional Families,* 2nd ed. Baltimore, Md.: Brookes Publishing Company, 1993.

Pueschel, S. M., P. S. Scola, L. E. Weidenman, and J. C. Bernier. *The Special Child: A Source Book for Parents of Children with Developmental Disabilities,* 2nd ed. Baltimore, Md.: Brookes Publishing Company, 1995.

Rapoport, Judith L. *The Boy Who Couldn't Stop Washing: The Experience and Treatment of Obsessive-Compulsive Disorder.* New York: Signet, 1991.

Seroussi, Karyn. *Unraveling the Mystery of Autism and Pervasive Developmental Disorder: A Mother's Story of Research and Recovery.* New York: Broadway Books, 2002.

Shaw, William, Ph.D. *Biological Treatments for Autism and PDD.* Toronto: Sunflower Publications, 2001.

Siegel, Lawrence M. *The Complete IEP Guide: How to Advocate for Your Special Ed Child,* 3rd ed. Berkeley, Calif.: NOLO, 2004.

Waltz, Mitzi. *Autistic Spectrum Disorders: Understanding the Diagnosis and Getting Help,* 2nd ed. Sebastopol, Calif.: Patient Center Guides, 2002.

Wilens, Timothy E. *Straight Talk About Psychiatric Medications for Kids,* revised ed. New York: Guilford Press, 2004.

Wright, Peter W. D., and Pamela Darr Wright. *Wrightslaw: From Emotions to Advocacy—The Special Education Survival Guide.* Hartfield, Va.: Harbor House Law Press, 2001.

———. *Wrightslaw: Special Education Law.* Hartfield, Va.: Harbor House Law Press, 1999.

There are hundreds of links to recommended websites, publications, books, screening tools, research studies, and organizations on the First Signs website, www.firstsigns.org. In addition, the following are especially recommended.

Screening Tools

The following developmental, autism, and Asperger syndrome/high-functioning autism screening tools have been reviewed against First Signs' screening criteria. Links to these screening tools are also provided at www.firstsigns.org.

Development Screening Tools

Ages & Stages Questionnaires® (ASQ): A Parent-Completed, Child-Monitoring System, 2nd ed. (ages 4 months to 6 years). Diane Bricker, Ph.D., and Jane Squires, Ph.D., with assistance from Linda Mounts, M.A., LaWanda Potter, M.S., Robert Nickel, M.D., Elizabeth Twombly, M.S., and Jane Farrell, M.S. Paul H. Brookes Publishing Company, Inc., P.O. Box 10624, Baltimore, MD 21285, (800) 638-3775, www.brookespublishing.com.

Communication and Symbolic Behavior Scales Developmental Profile (CSBS™ DP) (ages 6 to 24 months). Amy M. Wetherby, Ph.D., CCC-SLP, and Barry M. Prizant, Ph.D., CCC-SLP. Paul H. Brookes Publishing, Inc., P.O. Box 10624, Baltimore, MD 21285, (800) 638-3775, www.brooke spublishing.com.

Greenpsan Social-Emotional Growth Chart (ages 0 to 42 months). Stanley I. Greenspan, M.D. The Psychological Corp., Harcourt Assessment, 19500 Bulverde Road, San Antonio, TX 78259, (908) 397-7799, www.harcourt assessment.com.

Parents Evaluation of Developmental Status (PEDS) (ages 0 to 8 years). Frances Page Glascoe, Ph.D. Ellsworth and Vandermeer Press, LLC, P.O. Box 68164, Nashville, TN 37206, (615) 226-4460, (888) 729-1697, www.pedstest.com.

Autism Screening Tools

Modified Checklist for Autism in Toddlers (M-CHAT) (ages 16 to 48 months). Diana Robins, M.A., Deborah Fein, Ph.D., et al. Appears in "The Modified Checklist for Autism in Toddlers: An Initial Study Investigating the Early Detection of Autism and Pervasive Developmental Disorders." *Journal of Austim and Developmental Disorders* 31 (2), 131–44, and available through www.firstsigns.org.

Asperger Syndrome/High-Functioning Autism Screening Tools

Australian Scale for Asperger Syndrome (ASAS) (ages 5 and older). Michelle Garnet and Anthony J. Attwood, Ph.D. Queensland, Australia: School of Applied Psychology, Griffith University. See also www.asoak land.org/australian_scale_for_asperger.htm.

Autism Spectrum Screening Questionnaire (ASSQ) (ages 7 to 16). Stephen Ehlers, Ph.D., Christopher Gillberg, Ph.D., and Lorna Wing, Ph.D. Springer-Verlag New York Journal Fulfillment, P.O. Box 2485, Secaucus, NJ 07096, (201) 348-4033, www.springeronline.com.

Social Communication Questionnaire (SCQ) (formerly the Autism Screener Questionnaire (ASQ) (ages 4 and older). Michael Rutter, M.D., F.R.S., Anthony Bailey, M.D., and Catherine Lord, Ph.D. Western Psychological Services, 1203 Wilshire Blvd., Los Angeles, CA 90025-1251, (800) 648-8857 (U.S. and Canada only), (310) 478-2061, www.wpspublish.com.

Behavioral Screening Tools

Temperament and Behavior Scales (TABS) (ages 11 to 71 months). Paul H. Brookes Publishing, Inc., P.O. Box 10624, Baltimore, MD 21285, (800) 638-3775, www.brookespublishing.com.

Brief Infant-Toddler Social Emotional Assessment (BITSEA) (ages 12 to 36 months). Alice Carter and Margaret Briggs-Gowan. The Psychological Corp., Harcourt Assessment, 19500 Bulverde Road, San Antonio, TX 78259, (908) 397-7799, www.harcourtassessment.com.

ADHD Screening Tools

ADHD Symptom Checklist (ADHD-SC4) (ages 3 to 18). Kenneth Gadow and Joyce Spranfkin. Therapeutic Resource Company, P.O. Box 16814, Cleveland, OH 44116, (888) 331-7114 or (440) 331-7114, www.thera peuticresources.com.

Childhood Bipolar Screening Tools

Parent Version Young Mania Rating Scale (ages 5 to 15). This eleven-item scale is adapted from the clinical version of the Young Mania Rating Scale and is accessed online at http://www.healthyplace.com/communities/bipolar/p-ymrs.asp.

Recommended Publications

The Autism Perspective (TAP) magazine, 10153 Riverside Dr., Suite 243, Toluca Lake, CA 91602, (310) 709-0941, www.theautismperspective.org.

Exceptional Parent magazine, EP Global Communications, 551 Main St., Johnstown, PA 15901, (800) EPARENT (372-7368), www.exceptional parent.com.

Schafer Autism Report (free online newsletter), 9629 Old Placerville Rd., Sacramento, CA 95827, www.sarnet.org.

Organizations

American Academy of Pediatrics (AAP)
141 Northwest Point Blvd.
Elk Grove Village, IL 60007
(847) 434-4000
www.aap.org

Autism Research Institute (ARI)
4182 Adams Ave.
San Diego, CA 92116
(619) 563-6840 (fax)
www.autismwebsite.com/ari/index.htm

Autism Society of America
7910 Woodmont Ave., Suite 300
Bethesda, MD 20814-3067
(301) 657-0881
www.autism-society.org

Autism Speaks
610 Fifth Ave., Suite 604
New York, NY 10020
(212) 332-3580
www.autismspeaks.org

Cure Autism Now (CAN)
5455 Wilshire Blvd., Suite 715
Los Angeles, CA 90036
(888) 828-8476
www.canfoundation.org

Doug Flutie, Jr., Foundation for Autism
615 Concord St.
Framingham, MA 01702
(866)-3AUTISM
www.dougflutiejrfoundation.org

First Signs, Inc.
P.O. Box 358
Merrimac, MA 01860
(978) 346-4380
www.firstsigns.org

The Floortime Foundation
3213 Midfield Rd.
Baltimore, MD 21208
(443) 738-0807
www.floortime.org

**The Interdisciplinary Council on Learning and Developmental
Disorders (ICDL)**
4938 Hampden Lane, Suite 800
Bethesda, MD 20814
(301) 656-2667
www.icdl.com

**Medical Investigation of Neurodevelopmental Disorders, the
M.I.N.D. Institute**
2825 50th St.
Sacramento, CA 95817
(916) 703-0280
www.ucdmc.ucdavis.edu/mindinstitute/

National Alliance for Autism Research (NAAR)
99 Wall St., Research Park
Princeton, NJ 08540
(888) 777-NAAR
www.naar.org

**National Center for Birth Defects and Developmental Disabilities—
Autism Information Center**
Division of the Centers for Disease Control and Prevention (CDC)
www.cdc.gov/ncbddd/dd/ddautism.htm

**The National Center of Medical Home Initiatives for Children with
Special Needs**
141 Northwest Point Blvd.
Elk Grove Village, IL 60007
(847) 434-4000
www.medicalhomeinfo.org

Organization for Autism Research (OAR)
2111 Wilson Blvd., Suite 600
Arlington, VA 22201
(703) 351-5031
www.researchautism.org

Parents Action for Children (formerly, the I Am Your Child
Foundation)
1875 Connecticut Ave. NW, Suite 650
Washington, DC 20009
(202) 238-4878
www.iamyourchild.org

Unlocking Autism
P.O. Box 15388
Baton Rouge, LA 70895
(866) 366-3361
www.unlockingautism.org

Wrightslaw
Peter W. D. Wright and Pamela Darr Wright
Harbor House Law Press
P.O. Box 480
Hartfield, VA 23071
(804) 776-7605
www.wrightslaw.com

Zero to Three
National Center for Infants, Toddlers, and Families
2000 M St. NW, Suite 200
Washington, DC 20036
(202) 638-1144
www.zerotothree.org

Patient Education

American Academy of Child and Adolescent Psychiatry
3615 Wisconsin Ave. NW
Washington, DC 20016-3007
(202) 966-7300
www.aacap.org
Eighty-nine "Facts for Families" handouts may be downloaded for free.
Written in English, Spanish, and French, they address such topics as divorce,
disaster recovery, and how to choose a psychiatrist.

British Columbia Council for Families
204-2590 Granville St.
Vancouver, BC, Canada V6H 3H1
(604) 660-0675
www.bccf.bc.ca
Articles, online questionnaires, and links to resources on a variety of parenting and family topics. Carries individual and bulk copies of books and brochures on such topics as adolescence, marriage, family cohesion, and child development, as well as a parenting program, Nobody's Perfect.

Early Childhood Connections
The Centre for Community Child Health
6th Floor, South East Building
Royal Children's Hospital Melbourne
Flemington Road
Parkville, Victoria 3052 Australia
(03) 9345 5297
www.ecconnections.com.au
More than 700 international website links related to health and early childhood.

Kids Health
The Nemours Foundation
www.kidshealth.org/index2.html
Excellent information on health and safety, emotional and social development, and positive parenting.

Medem Smart Parents' Health Source
Medem, Inc.
649 Mission St., 2nd Floor
San Francisco, CA 94105
(415) 644-3800
www.medem.com/medlb/medlb_msphs.cfm
Medem is a Web library of health information from a variety of medical societies, including the American Academy of Pediatrics.

National Early Childhood Technical Assistance Center (NECTAC)
Campus Box 8040, UNC
Chapel Hill, NC 27599-8040
(919) 962-2001
www.nectac.org/about/staff.asp
Supports implementation of the early childhood provisions of the Individuals with Disabilities Education Act (IDEA).

National Library of Medicine
National Institutes of Health
8600 Rockville Pike
Bethesda, MD 20894
www.nlm.nih.gov/
World's largest biomedical library.

South Australian Department of Human Services
295 South Terrace
Adelaide, South Australia 5000
Parent Helpline 1300 364 100
www.cyh.sa.gov.au
Extremely rich information for parents on a huge range of psychosocial issues concerning teens and young children.

for accompanying health problems,
161–64, 175–76, 177–79
alternative approaches vs.
mainstream types of, 183
applied behavioral analysis, 37,
108, 185–86
behavioral approaches in, 185–86
biomedical types of, 188–89
case histories of, 170–80, 192–95
clinical types of, 186–87
as cure vs. mitigation, 159–60, 224
developmental approaches in,
184–85
early intervention recommended
for, 23–27, 28, 30, 87–88
efficacy of, 8, 26–27, 28, 37–38,
39
evaluation guidelines for, 181–83
financial costs of, 95, 180, 191,
214, 220
Floortime (therapy), 8, 27, 59, 89,
134, 152–53, 168, 171, 172–73,
174, 184, 243
government services in, 30,
93–102, 106–8, 111–12, 183,
220
health insurance coverage of,
101–3, 112
minimum schedules recommended
for, 169, 173
for older children, 27–28
one-on-one, 166
organizational approaches in, 186
parental discoveries of modes of,
156–57
placebo effect of, 181
professional review of, 169
research program enrollments for,
191
school system services in, 97–100,
103–5, 107–8, 111, 157, 183,
223–25
selection process for, 165–83
team coordination in, 90–93
varieties of, 184–90
See also developmental disorders

Barbera, Lucas, 53, 114, 160, 226
Barbera, Mary, 53, 114, 160, 226

Bauer, Andy, 13
Bauer, Kathy, 13, 96, 226
Bauman, Margaret, 26
behavioral optometry, 187
behavioral screening tools, 241
behavior disorders, 67, 79, 84
behavior therapy, 89, 185–86
Bell, Peter, 30, 229
bipolar disorder, 78–79, 125, 126,
133, 241
blood tests, 74, 117
Bock, Kenneth, 163–64
Boy Who Loved Windows, The (Stacey),
26–27
brain development
critical first three years of, 21–24
lifetime process of, 27
brain disorders, 84–85
brain injury, 126, 132
Brazelton, T. Berry, 15, 51
breathing exercise, 154
Brookes Publishing, 67
brushing program, 169
Building Healthy Minds (Greenspan),
51

casein, 38, 163
Cather, Karin, 34, 144, 150, 152,
212
Cather, Noah, 149, 212
Centers for Disease Control (CDC),
2
cerebral palsy, 42, 84
chelation, 179, 188
Childhood Autism Rating Scale
(CARS), 107–8
childhood bipolar disorder, 78–79,
125, 126, 133, 241
childhood disintegrative disorder,
130
child psychiatrists/psychologists, 85,
114
Child with Special Needs, The
(Greenspan and Wieder), 27,
59, 134
circles of communication, 172–73,
175, 203
cognitive development, 41
Cohen, Arlene, 206

medications, 176–77, 188
mental retardation, 7, 28, 30, 42, 67, 122–23, 129, 131, 132
mercury poisoning, 164, 179, 188
Meyer, Don, 219
milk, 163, 178
mind, theory of, 25
Modified Checklist for Autism in Toddlers (M-CHAT), 75–77, 240
mood disorders, 7, 133
mood regulation, medication for, 176–77
motor skills
  developmental milestones in, 41–42
  therapy choices vs., 166, 167, 187
  therapy on, 88, 89
multidisciplinary evaluation (MDE), 115–22
music therapy, 189
mutism, 133
myelination, 24

name, child's response to, 36, 46, 48, 54, 69
narrative play therapy, 175
Naseef, Robert, 148, 211–12
National Academy of Sciences, 169
National Early Childhood Technical Assistance Center, 93
National Library of Medicine, 141, 247
neural connections, 21, 24
neurologists, 84–85, 88
nonverbal learning disorder, 132
nutritional supplementation, 177–78, 188

Oberleitner, Robby, 34, 106–9, 200
Oberleitner, Ron, 106–9
Oberleitner, Sharon, 34, 106–9, 200, 228
object use, 69
obsessive-compulsive disorder, 125, 126, 133
occupational therapists (OTs), 88–89, 187
occupational therapy, 101, 166, 167
O'Connor, Alexander, 31

O'Connor, Julia, 31
Olsen, Ashley, 208
Olsen, Mary-Kate, 208
oppositional defiant disorder, 133
Ordinary Families, Special Children (Seligman and Darling), 212
orthoptic therapy, 187

Palmieri, Ida, 145, 170, 213
Palmieri, Michael, 145, 170, 213
PANDAS (pediatric autoimmune neuropsychiatric disorders associated with streptococcal infections), 125, 133, 177
parents
  advocacy role of, 19, 55, 57–59, 99–100, 103–5, 221–29
  concerned outsider's approach to, 56–57
  denial responses of, 31–35, 55
  developmental screening tools administered by, 65, 67–70
  in diagnostic process, 11–14, 20, 29–30, 57–59, 128–29, 139–40
  disagreements between, 33–34, 215
  fears experienced by, 80–81
  goals set by, 199–205
  individual counseling for, 147–49
  marital relationship of, 174, 211–16
  nurturing connection maintained by, 152–53
  personal support for, 82–83, 112, 215–16
  relaxation breaks for, 149–52, 154, 213, 214
  rights of, 18, 223
  self-education efforts of, 139, 140–43
  siblings' differences addressed by, 216–19
  single, 215
  stress endured by, 147–48, 154, 180, 211–12
  in support groups, 143–47
  therapeutic solutions discovered by, 156–57
  will in event of death of, 220

About the Author

Nancy D. Wiseman is the founder and president of First Signs, Inc., a national nonprofit organization dedicated to educating professionals and parents about early identification and intervention for children with autism and other developmental disorders. Nancy has been dedicated to all aspects of the organization's development since its inception in 1999. Though there are many organizations, national and local, focused on research, treatment, and public awareness of autism and other developmental disorders, First Signs has created a unique niche specific to early identification and intervention. Before devoting herself to First Signs, Nancy worked in corporate communications for over twenty years building brand awareness, educating the public, and creating major marketing campaigns for international companies in the financial, travel, office products, computer, and software industries.

Nancy is also the mother of a child diagnosed with autism. She knows firsthand how difficult it is to unravel complex issues, find the right treatments for children, and learn what questions to ask, how to persist, and where to go for answers. She has counseled thousands of parents nationwide on how to navigate the process. Her organization's nationwide public awareness and training program, along with their award-winning website and video, screening kit, and other materials, is unique in its approach. Nancy has been interviewed by a variety of print and television media, including *USA Today, Parents* magazine, and NBC's *Today* show.